THE VIRTUAL REFERENCE DESK

Creating a Reference Future

Edited by

R. David Lankes   Eileen G. Abels

Marilyn Domas White   Saira N. Haque

facet publishing

Published by
Facet Publishing
7 Ridgmount Street
London WC1E 7AE

Facet Publishing is wholly owned by CILIP: the Chartered Institute of Library and Information Professionals.

First published in the USA by Neal-Schuman Publishers, Inc., 2006.

British Library Cataloguing in Publication Data
A catalogue record for this book is available from the British Library.

ISBN-1-85604-566-8

Printed and bound in the United States of America.

Contents

List of Figures   v

List of Tables   vii

Introduction   ix
Eileen G. Abels

Acknowledgments   xiii

Part I: Creating a Reference Future: Chat Reference   1

1. Bringing Together Teens and Chat Reference: Reconsidering "The Match Made in Heaven"   3
Laura Kortz, Sharon Morris, and Louise W. Greene

2. Investigating Interpersonal Communication in Chat Reference: Dealing with Impatient Users and Rude Encounters   23
Marie L. Radford

Part II: Creating a Reference Future: Training and Staffing   47

3. Training for Online Virtual Reference: Measuring Effective Techniques   49
Eileen G. Abels and Malissa Ruffner

4. Staffing for Live Electronic Reference: Balancing Service and Sacrifice   75
Joe Blonde

Part III: Creating a Reference Future: Evaluation   89

5. Establishing Performance Targets for a Virtual Reference Service: Counting Totals and Beyond   91
Deb Hutchison and Michele Pye

6. Creating the Infrastructure for Digital Reference   109
    Research: Examining the Digital Reference
    Electronic Warehouse (DREW) Project
    Scott Nicholson and R. David Lankes

**Part IV: Creating a Reference Future: Innovative   131
    Approaches**

7. Managing a Full-Scale, 24/7, Reference Service   133
    Consortium: Integrating Specialists from Public
    and Academic Libraries
    Vera Daugaard, Morten Fogh, and Ellen Nielsen

8. Creating a Knowledge Base: Analyzing a Veteran   155
    Reference Librarian's Brain
    Charles Early, Andrea Japzon, and Sarah Endres

9. Building Wi-Fi Technology and a New Mobile   169
    Service Model: Creating Change in Information
    Service Delivery at the Orange County (Florida)
    Library System
    Kathryn Robinson

10. Building a Virtual Community: Repurposing   193
    Professional Tools for Team-Based Experiential
    Learning
    Karen Wenk

Conclusion: Looking to the Future   203
Marilyn Domas White

Index   209
About the Editors   219
About the Contributors   221

List of Figures

7-1. Screen Shot of Biblioteksvagten Service   135
8-1. Search Results for the Keyword *Standards*   162
8-2. Example of a Database Entry   163
9-1. Reference Questions Decline While Directional   172
      Questions Increase
9-2. Overall Reference Questions Declining While   175
      Directional Questions Soaring at Branches
9-3. The "Before" Picture   178
9-4. Use of Wireless Communication Badge for   179
      Customer Service
9-5. Vocera Communications Network   180
9-6. Use of PDAs in Service Delivery   181
9-7. QuestLine Manager using OLIVE and Online   183
      Resources to Assist Customers
9-8. The Customer's View of OLIVE   184
9-9. Greeting and Determining the Customer's Needs   188
9-10. Walk-in and Virtual Service is a Work in Progress   189
10-1. Communication within the Virtual Collaboratory   200

List of Tables

2-1. Client Relational Barriers (N=245)   30

2-2. Example of Closing Problems Subtheme of Barriers   31

2-3. Example of Relational Disconnect/Failure to Build Rapport Subtheme   33

2-4. Example of Relational Disconnect/Failure to Build Rapport Subtheme   34

2-5. Example of Relational Disconnect/Failure to Build Rapport Subtheme   36

3-1. Overview of Course Modules, Objectives, and Activities   54

3-2. Opportunities for Interaction with Other Workshop Participants   58

3-3. Enrollment and Completion of Exercises and Assessments   60

3-4. Participant Satisfaction with Various Aspects of the Workshop   64

3-5. Satisfaction with Cheat Sheets and Online Tutorials   65

3-6. Confidence in Ability to Conduct a Virtual Reference Interview   66

4-1. Type of Service   78

4-2. Hours of Coverage for Individual Libraries   79

4-3. Hours of Coverage for Libraries in Consortia   80

4-4. Staff Categories   82

5-1. Participating Libraries   97

5-2. Setting Performance Targets: Sample Grid   98

5-3. How Did VPL Measure Up?   105

6-1. Percentage of Respondents Using Each Reference Tool (N=53)   115

6-2. Formats of Final Resolution of Reference Transactions (N=53)   116

6-3. Percentage of Services Currently Collecting   117
      Specified Fields (N=53)
6-4. Percentage of Services Currently Collecting   120
      or Willing to Collect Specified Fields (N=53)
9-1. Population Growth for Orange County, Florida   171
9-2. Shift in Percentage of Questions Answered at   173
      Main

Introduction

Eileen G. Abels

The VRD (Virtual Reference Desk) Conference is designed to stimulate sharing of the most current research, practices, and ideas in digital reference. The fifth annual conference, "Creating a Reference Future," focused on the effects of the increasing integration of digital reference with traditional reference. It also explored the management issues accompanying these changes. This book, *The Virtual Reference Desk: Creating a Reference Future*, reflects the best of the conference. Its four parts correspond to the four major themes: chat reference, training and staffing, evaluation, and innovative service approaches. The contributors of the ten chapters all work on the front lines as public, academic, and special librarians or as library and information science (LIS) educators. They have updated their original presentations for publication in this book.

Part I, "Creating a Reference Future: Chat Reference," offers two chapters examining different aspects of this age group as users of virtual reference services. Until instant messaging gained huge popularity, young people did not use traditional reference services heavily. Now they are drawn to chat reference since it is compatible with their preferred communication style.

Chapter 1, "Bringing Together Teens and Chat Reference: Reconsidering 'The Match Made in Heaven,'" spotlights key information behaviors and recommends novel ways to provide the most effective service. The authors, Laura Kortz, Sharon Morris, and Louise W. Greene, describe the challenges of chat reference services in three different states. They incorporate various sources—including a literature review and the findings of a report from a focus on group encounter.

In Chapter 2, "Investigating Interpersonal Communication in Chat Reference: Dealing with Impatient Users and Rude Encounters," Marie L. Radford reports on an in-depth qualitative analysis of 245 chat transcripts and suggests ways for practitioners to employ the most useful communication techniques to deal with rude and impatient clients—many presumed to be teens.

Part II, "Creating a Reference Future: Training and Staffing," considers critical management concerns as many libraries deal with the desire to increase reference services and the reality of trying to accomplish this goal without adding staff.

Chapter 3, "Training for Online Virtual Reference: Measuring Effective Techniques," by Eileen G. Abels and Malissa Ruffner, tackles important questions: How should we combine the use of technology, reference, and communication skills to meet the particular challenges of chat reference training? Is it feasible to teach chat reference skills in an online environment? How successful are online training techniques, especially the ones from the increasingly popular consortia, where librarians work for the same global chat service?

In Chapter 4, "Staffing for Live Electronic Reference: Balancing Service and Sacrifice," Joe Blonde surveys best practices and essential issues in his assessment of 16 Canadian academic libraries. He explains the importance of understanding the issues and exploring various models as chat reference becomes fully integrated into staffing basic reference services.

Part III, "Creating a Reference Future: Evaluation," contains two chapters on how to measure successes and failures. The first chapter describes a specific effort to develop metrics; the second presents an idea intended to assist in collaborative evaluation efforts.

Chapter 5, "Establishing Performance Targets for a Virtual Reference Service: Counting Totals and Beyond," by Deb Hutchison and Michele Pye, evaluates the results of a literature review and a survey of staff from 14 North American public libraries offering chat services. Noting the lack of guidance in the literature to support in the development of strong metrics, they establish benchmarks and develop performance targets for virtual reference service.

In Chapter 6, "Creating the Infrastructure for Digital Reference Research: Examining the Digital Reference Electronic Warehouse (DREW) Project," Scott Nicholson and R. David Lankes address the lack of metrics for chat reference. They recommend the creation of a Digital Reference Electronic Warehouse (DREW). This large database of reference transactions would provide a data source and provide an opportunity to create tools for measurement and evaluation that could go beyond one library or one consortium.

Part IV, "Creating a Reference Future: Innovative Approaches," concentrates on the successful strategies libraries have utilized to meet the information needs of today's information seekers. These chapters illustrate how to think outside the box by thinking beyond the physical reference desk and the library building. The four chapters include a multilibrary-type collaboration, mobile librarians, a knowledge base to capture a librarian's tacit knowledge, and a virtual collaboratory.

Chapter 7, "Managing a Full-Scale, 24/7, Reference Service Consortium: Integrating Specialists from Public and Academic Libraries," by Vera Daugaard, Morten Fogh, and Ellen Nielsen studies the experiences of Danish collaboration between public and academic libraries to offer a single service called Biblioteksvagten. This serves the information needs of the citizens of Denmark by drawing from more than 250 librarians in more than 50 different libraries. The effort demonstrates a successful cooperation among libraries of all types and sizes to meet the needs of the citizenry. The conclusions will prove valuable to others who may consider developing a similar multitype library.

Chapter 8, "Creating a Knowledge Base: Analyzing a Veteran Reference Librarian's Brain," tries to solve a problem common to many libraries: how might one identify, codify, and make available the tacit knowledge of a skilled reference librarian for use in answering general questions. This chapter presents an innovative solution to creating a knowledge base to enhance service provision, training efforts, and evaluation. It explores how a novice reference librarian might utilize both the chat and e-mail reference questions of a seasoned librarian to build a knowledge base. This dynamic tool improves reference services by raising awareness of resources used to fulfill information requests and provides a training tool for new librarians.

Chapter 9, "Building Wi-Fi Technology and a New Mobile Service Model: Creating Change in Information Service Delivery at the Orange County (Florida) Library System," by Kathryn Robinson, describes the use of a combination of wireless technologies to enhance reference service by allowing librarians to provide in-library service beyond the reference desk. The new technology complements an already wide array of existing services that include telephone, e-mail and chat reference services, a drive-through service, home delivery of materials, streaming video, and in-person classes. The efforts made by this library system focus on customer needs and are responsive to changing lifestyles, yet, at the same time, provide efficient and cost-effective services.

Chapter 10, "Building a Virtual Community: Repurposing Professional Tools for Team-Based Experiential Learning," by Karen Wenk, looks at an enterprise being developed at Rutgers University Libraries called a virtual collaboratory, combining collaboration space and laboratory, and innovatively using faculty, subject librarians, and business partners in the community. The collaboratory introduces features not available in existing commercial course-management software and provides a laboratory, meeting place, and workspace using open source software. This type of environment is applicable to interdisciplinary teams in other settings.

The Conclusion, "Looking to the Future" by Marilyn Domas White, reviews the chapters and marks areas that will continue to intrigue and challenge.

Although the contributors to *The Virtual Reference Desk: Creating a Reference Future* represent many different facets of cutting-edge thought, they all share the same keen interest in the success of reference services in the future. They are committed to the idea that reference services must evolve to continue to meet the needs of users. Throughout these pages, these contributors are most certainly "Creating a Reference Future."

Acknowledgments

The editors would like to thank everyone who contributed to the planning and success of the Virtual Reference Desk Conference and to the development of this book. In particular, we would like to thank the conference sponsors: The U.S. Department of Education, Online Computer Library Center (OCLC), Syracuse University's School of Information Studies, and ALA Reference and User Services Association (RUSA). OCLC's George Needham, Nancy Lensenmayer, Donna Gehring, Mary Ann Semigel; Steve Leonard; and RUSA's Carol Tobin deserve a special mention.

In addition, without those at the Information Institute of Syracuse, the conference, *The Virtual Reference Desk: Creating a Reference Future* would not be possible. These people include Blythe Bennett, Jo Ann Cortez, Joann Wasik, and Brian Quackenbush.

Thank you to the speakers, presenters, panel participants, and attendees, who all provided a valuable contribution to the conference and ongoing dialogue.

And last, but certainly not least, thanks to those who assisted in the preparation of the book on the staff of the Information Institute of Syracuse and the staff at Neal-Schuman Publishers, in particular to Michael Kelley the development and production editor.

The editors are grateful to the many people who have contributed to the success of the conference and the publication of this book.

PART I

Creating a Reference Future: Chat Reference

Chapter 1

Bringing Together Teens and Chat Reference: Reconsidering "The Match Made in Heaven"

*Laura Kortz, Sharon Morris,
and Louise W. Greene*

OVERVIEW

Although teenagers constitute a large user group for many library chat reference services, little attention has been paid to their use of these services. To fill this gap, we present an overview of teen use of chat-reference services based on our experiences providing chat reference service at three statewide services. Starting with a brief look at teen development and how teens are using the Internet, we go on to provide statistics about teen use of chat reference services as well as focus-group data, sample transcripts, and survey comments. We conclude by offering general guidelines for communicating with teens online and providing suggestions for future research.

INTRODUCTION

Since the late 1990s, libraries have experimented with technology to provide traditional library services in the online environment. The use of e-mail, chat, and other online media to provide

reference services has presented numerous challenges and opportunities as well as unexpected additions to traditional library service models (Coffman and Arrett, 2004). Collaborative
statewide services like New Jersey's QandA NJ, Colorado's
AskColorado, and Maryland's AskUsNow! were developed in
part to enable libraries of all types to provide chat reference
while sharing the considerable cost of staffing and software.
Collaborative online reference services have brought together
librarians from different environments, including public, academic, and special libraries. As a result of these collaborations,
librarians must often work with users outside of their primary
patron base. This means that academic and adult services librarians, who are unaccustomed to working with teens, must
deal with their increasing presence in chat reference services.
These librarians are sometimes shocked and insulted by teen
online behavior, and it is in partly with these librarians in mind
that we have undertaken this report.

Although studies of teen use of online technologies such
as instant messaging (IM) and chat rooms are beginning to
appear more frequently in journals in several fields within the
social sciences, no studies of teen use of chat reference services
have been published. Our aim is to present a descriptive overview of teen use of these services in order to stimulate further
research.

Our observations and impressions of chat reference with
teens are drawn from our daily experiences staffing "online reference desks" at three statewide chat reference services. Each
of us has staffed an "online reference desk" for nearly two
years. Since we participate in very busy services, we have participated in a total of over 3,000 chats during this time. Because
we have participated in so many interactions from multiple locations, we feel confident that our observations are indicative
of chat reference use around the country. Our goal in writing
this is to help librarians understand and appreciate teen chat
reference users, to present practical tools for serving this population and to stimulate further discussion and inquiry into teen
use of chat reference services. We believe that responsive service to this population is crucial to the future development and
growth of chat reference services.

ADOLESCENT DEVELOPMENT

The Young Adult Library Services Association's (YALSA) *Competencies for Librarians Serving Youth* (YALSA, 2003) lists "knowledge of client group" as an important competency for librarians who work with teens. Knowledge of client group involves acquiring and applying "factual and interpretative information on youth development, development assets, and popular culture in planning for materials, services and programs for young adults." Because teens constitute a majority of virtual reference service users, it is not only helpful but necessary for librarians who staff these services to have a basic knowledge of teen development. But understanding teens can be difficult because, as Csikszentmihalyi and Larson (1984) have noted, adolescence is one of the hardest periods to characterize. The moment one makes a generalization about it, an opposite statement, equally true, often comes to mind. Change and contradiction seem inherent to this life stage, and adolescents who are nasty and rude one minute can be helpful and appreciative the next. This experimentation with roles, perspectives, and possible selves seems to be crucial to development during the teen years. (Csikszentmihalyi and Larson, 1984).

Steinberg (1998) offers a good summary of the physical, cognitive, emotional, and social changes experienced during this life stage. Physical changes include the growth spurt and puberty, which is triggered by changes in hormonal levels: estrogen in girls and testosterone in boys. Cognitive changes include the ability to think about possibilities and look ahead to the future, the ability to think abstractly, to think about thinking, to look at issues from multiple perspectives, and to consider issues from a relative rather than absolute perspective. Emotional changes include less reliance on parents and greater reliance on peers. Adolescent relationships become more complicated, deeper, and more intimate than those of children. Teens become more sophisticated emotionally and spend more time thinking about their feelings and those of others. Adolescence also heralds the beginning of romantic and sexual relationships. Socially teens begin to prepare for more mature roles, including joining the work force or preparing for careers through educational preparation.

The developmental changes cited above seem to engender more sophisticated information-seeking behavior among teens. Teen chats with librarians are far more sophisticated that those of children, for instance. Also, as teens mature into young adults and more is expected of them at school, work, and in their relationships, their need for information increases and becomes more complex. Recent research in neuroscience seems to indicate that some of the changes in teen behavior and thinking may be linked to changes taking place in the brain prior to and during adolescence, all the way into the early 20s. While a discussion of these neural changes is beyond the scope of this paper, we refer librarians interested in the "teen brain" to the work of Giedd (1996) and others at the National Institutes of Mental Health (2004), Strauch (2003), and PBS Frontline (2002) for further information on this promising area of research.

TEENS AND THE INTERNET

If we define teenagers as persons between the ages of 12 and 18, the latest census (U.S. Census Bureau, 2000) counted about 30 million teenagers in the United States. It is difficult to know exactly how many of these teens are online because not all reports use the same ages to define teenager. In 2001, the Bureau of Labor Statistics surveyed 56,000 households and found that 85% of 18–24-year-olds, 75% of 14–17-year-olds, and 65% of 10–13-year-olds use the Internet (National Telecommunications and Information Administration, 2002). Two years later, however, the UCLA Internet Report (2003) surveyed a much smaller sample , 2,000 households, and reported that 97% of teens 12–18 were online either at home or school. The current generation of teenagers is the first in history to live their entire lives with personal computers and the Internet. They have grown up with communication technologies such as e-mail, cell phones, chat, instant messaging, and text messaging, prompting some authors to say they were "born with the chip" (Abram and Luther, 2004). Because the "Millennials," as they are sometimes called, have grown up with computers, the Internet, and other communication technologies, it is no surprise that they are the majority group of chat reference users.

Much of what we know about teen Internet usage comes from reports of the Pew Internet and American Life Project (2001). The Project conducted a survey of 754 teens and their parents to determine how teens were using the Internet and what effects their usage had on their families and social lives. What the researchers discovered was not surprising: teens use the Internet to complete homework assignments, to keep in touch with friends, to make new friends, and for recreational and commercial purposes, buying music, books, clothing, and other items. Of the teens surveyed, 74% used instant messaging (IM) and of this group nearly all used it at least once a week. IM and e-mail were cited as important to their social lives: 48% reported that the Internet improved their relationship with friends, and 32% said the Internet had helped them make new friends. Since friendships are especially important during adolescence, and the influence of peers is considerable, it follows that teens have adopted IM for social use. But the Internet has also become important for educational purposes. The researchers found that 94% of online teens reported using the Internet to conduct research for school, and 71% said they relied mostly on Internet sources for the last big project they did for school (Pew, 2001).

While we have a good idea of how teens are using the Internet, researchers are just beginning to look at how Internet use affects teen development. Subrahmanyam and colleagues (2001) reviewed research on the impact of teen computer use on cognitive skills, academic and social development, relationships, and perceptions of reality. More recently Subrahmanyam, Greenfield, and Tynes (2004) have begun to investigate teen use of chat rooms as a window into teenage sexuality and identity development. Other authors have studied teens who form close relationships online (Wolak et al., 2003), discussions of race and ethnicity in teen chat rooms (Tynes, Reynolds, and Greenfield, 2004), and linguistic and communication patterns in teen chat rooms (Greenfield and Subrahmanyam, 2003).

Maczewski (2002) interviewed nine teens aged 13 to 19 about their Internet use and found three themes: the notion of "wowness"; experiences of freedom, power, and connectedness; and exploration of self and identities through virtual relationships.

The teens in her study described being online as powerful and exciting. They enjoyed being able to experiment with different identities. They valued the anonymity, connectivity, and inter-activity of the medium, which made this experimentation possi-ble. Merchant (2001) studied six teen girls who used IM regularly and described them as innovators. To demonstrate some of their innovations with language, he described the now familiar fea-tures of chat: abbreviations, phonetic spelling, emoticons, and numeric and alphabetic combinations (e.g., b4 for before, ne1 for anyone).

Boneva and colleagues (in press) have also studied teen com-munication in IM and discovered that one of the features that most appeals to teens is the ability to multitask and to commu-nicate with several people simultaneously. Most of the teens they interviewed used IM primarily to chat with friends they knew in real life, and their conversations were about what had hap-pened at school that day, hobbies, and social activities. It is clear from these studies that e-mail, IM, and chat rooms have become integral components of teens' social lives, so it is no wonder that several collaborative chat reference services throughout the country report high use of their services by teens. Librarians may want to familiarize themselves with these studies because it is likely that users of their services are also using IM and chat rooms, and knowledge of patterns of use and teen communica-tion styles may help librarians provide better service.

TEENS AND CHAT REFERENCE: USAGE

Throughout the country, many collaborative virtual reference services report heavy teen use. In Colorado, the AskColorado chat reference service determined that 56% of their total use in the 2003–2004 school year was by K-12 students. In the 2004–2005 school year, teen use of the service has continued to con-stitute more than 50% of total use. The largest percentage of school-age users are middle school students: seventh and eighth graders together account for over 50% of total K-12 usage of the service (AskColorado, 2005).

In 2004, Vince Mariner, from Florida's statewide service Ask A Librarian, reported that the Florida Virtual School, an online high school, comprised 9% of their total use (personal correspondence). This illustrates that students using online alternative education are not only drawn to online library services, but may rely heavily on these services, if no physical libraries are available to them.

Two of the largest collaborative online-reference services in the country also report heavy teen use. Maryland's AskUsNow! receives an average of 4,000 questions per month, and 38% of these questions come from teenagers (Thompson, 2004, personal communication). In New Jersey, QandA NJ receives about 6,000 questions per month, and between 50–60% of these questions are asked by teenagers (Sweet, 2004, personal communication).

Although teens use these services heavily, we have no idea how they perceive them, how they discover them, and what meaning they might have in their lives. Qualitative research in this area would be invaluable and might prove useful for garnering funding to ensure sustainability.

TEENS AND CHAT REFERENCE: FOCUS-GROUP DATA

Despite the growing number of studies conducted in other fields, no studies have been conducted to examine teen use and perceptions of chat reference services. In order to gather preliminary data for such a study, Greene and Thompson (2004) conducted a pilot focus group and usability study designed to gather general data about teens' use of technology and gauge their impressions of library chat reference services. The methodology used was a combination of usability testing and focus-group discussion. Five college-bound teenagers who had recently graduated from high school met with the researchers to discuss their Internet habits. Following discussion, they each were shown the chat reference service of the college they would be attending and used the service to ask a question. After the teens had explored their colleges' chat reference services, the group met again to discuss their experiences.

All five teenagers said they began research for school assignments on the Internet rather than going to the library. They reported checking several sites to gather ideas and looked for credible as well as expedient information. They looked for opportunities to cut and paste, reducing the amount of original work they would need to complete.

All five teenagers were regular users of IM and chat rooms. When asked what they liked about these media, they said that anonymity was an important component of their online inter-actions. They also liked the ability to have multiple screen names and to hold simultaneous conversations. Other studies have reported that teens like to multitask: as one teen said, he liked "always being on without dead air." They also reported that they enjoyed the casual nature of chat and the use of jargon, abbreviations, and coded messages.

Although all the teens in the group used the Internet to search for information and were IM and chat proficient, none had ever used a chat reference service. The focus group format provided a unique opportunity in which to gather first impressions of new users. At first, the teens did not understand that a live librarian would be helping them in real-time. When the synchronous nature of the service was explained, they questioned why the library would have staff members "waiting around" to answer questions. One teen asked, "Don't the librarians have other things they need to be doing?" They also expressed curiosity about the librarians at the other end and wondered what they might be doing while waiting to answer questions. They wondered who was at the other end and what he or she was like. They also ex-pressed curiosity about who would be reading their question.

After the researchers provided a brief explanation of chat reference and answered the teens' questions, each teen used the service at the library of the college they would be attending in the fall. These were their impressions:

- They expressed a preference for chat reference over e-mail reference.
- They valued the ability to remain anonymous and ap-preciated not having to provide an e-mail address.
- They recommended highlighting the option to remain anonymous.
- They expressed a desire for greater speed and wanted op-tions; for instance, they wanted to be able to chose between web-based chat interface and a text message interface.

- They expressed a preference for personalizing the service by being able to develop a virtual relationship with a librarian.
- They wanted the ability to request a specific librarian (who had been helpful in a prior session), and, at the same time, they wanted to be able to avoid librarians they felt had not been helpful.
- They wanted the option to rate librarians and felt this might be an incentive for better service.

By the end of the discussion, the teens understood that chat reference services might be helpful to them in their college careers and said they would very likely use them again. However, since they had not known about them prior to the focus group session, they recommended more aggressive marketing. Because of the limited sample size, the findings cannot be generalized. However, several of their comments are consistent with prior research on the habits of this generation: preference for anonymity, experimentation with multiple identities by taking different user names, and multitasking as well as a preference for doing research on the Internet rather than in libraries. Focus groups can be a powerful way to gather information about user experiences and might be a catalyst for service improvements (Massey-Burzio, 1998).

TEEN USE OF CHAT REFERENCE SERVICES

The teens in the Greene and Thompson study were first-time users of a chat reference service, but thousands of teens around the country use these services regularly. The Library Research Services sent outcome surveys of users of AskColorado. The Library Research Services is a unit of the Colorado State Library which surveyed Colorado's state service. Of the respondents who indicated that they were under the age of 18, 71% used the virtual reference service to research homework assignments and other school projects, and 29% reported that they learned more about a skill, hobby, or other personal interest (Lance and Dickerson, 2005). Our own informal review of chat reference transcripts from the Colorado, Maryland, and New Jersey services indicate four major categories of questions:

- homework and research
- personal and recreational
- inappropriate and prank
- crisis or "cry for help"

In the following section, we will address these and provide transcript examples to illustrate each category.

Homework and Research

Homework and research questions is the largest category of questions asked by teens. Based on a rough tabulation of transcripts from each of our services, we have found that homework questions account for about 75–85% of questions asked by teens. Teens ask homework questions about the wide range of subjects taught at the middle and high school levels. They may seek research assistance, help with narrowing down a topic and selecting appropriate resources, assistance with citation styles, or simple need specific information to complete a project. Here are some sample homework questions (with original spelling and punctuation):

> What are the 3 parts of the National Security Strategy of the United States?
>
> What is the difference between sunlight and artificial light when using a spectroscope?
>
> i need a BRIEF descripton of the french revolution
>
> can you give me a classic outline of the story the bluest eye
>
> I'm not very good at doing bibliographys. I was wondering if someone could please help me.
>
> I want to know if you boil water in a tea kettle and steam starts to come out is that a physical change or a chemical change?

Librarians working with teens on homework questions may simply assist by finding a fact or may provide instruction on using online databases and other library resources and services. In some cases, librarians will refer teens to their local libraries. In many cases, students appreciate being helped online. Below are anonymous comments from students who had been helped by an online librarian (and completed an exit survey):

> "Tracy, the librarian, helped me a lot with my project and I appreciate her help so much! Thanks again!"
>
> "I am out of my wits to the end thanks to C.J., who helped much better than I would do alone for research. Thank you very much!"
>
> "This program is very helpful and I am finally glad there is something that can help me get my homework done way quicker than just by searching google for hours on end. Thanks!"
>
> "This was very very helpful and a great idea to help students obtain homework help."
>
> "I love this program it made my homework go by faster"
>
> "I have fonud this service VERY helpful and useful on several occasions with English,History, and Math questions. The librarians are very helpful, and if they cannot find an answer, they give me another resource that will help me. This service is VERY useful and VERY helpful."

These randomly selected comments illustrate common reasons teen students appreciate virtual reference services: the helpful nature of the librarian, the assistance they receive with homework research, and the fact that the service reduces the time they spend searching for information. It is interesting to note that although this generation is widely perceived to be technology savvy, that they still appreciate help from a professional when conducting research online.

At their best, virtual reference transactions with teenagers are productive and conducive to learning. But at other times, the match is not always made in heaven. Students who expect instant service are sometimes disappointed when the librarian cannot deliver. For example, the following section of a transcript illustrates a homework question that posed a challenge:

> Teenager: Can you help me answer a question?
> Teenager: hi
> Librarian: Hi (teenager's name). What's your question? I'll
>   try:)
> Teenager: can you help me find the food,clothing,work,beliefs,shelter,recreation,and tools for Tanzania

Librarian: Wow! That's a tall order! Have you looked anywhere yet?
Teenager: yes but i really could not find anything
Librarian: Okay. What is your deadline and are you writing
   a report?
Teenager: my deadline is to finish by tonight and no just
   write the facts
Teenager: how fast do you think you can find the info because i have to get ready to hit the sack
Librarian: Okay. I am going to see what I can find. Watch
   your screen......And after we stop our session,you will
   automatically receive an email that reminds you of
   web pages we visited, okay?

As the above transcript shows, students may wait until the
last minute to seek assistance. Some students expect the librarian to be able to provide instant answers. When librarians
cannot meet these expectations, students can become impatient,
disappointed, and just plain rude. As Radford and Thompson
(2004) have noted, it is important that librarians not take this
behavior personally. Librarians should attempt to empathize
with student's frustration and do what they can to provide assistance. Another scenario similar to the last minute assignment,
is the one in which the student must have information immediately and types "hurry, hurry" several times. Librarians at
QandA NJ deal with this behavior by letting the student know
how long the interaction will take and giving them an option
of coming back later when they have more time. It is helpful
sometimes to ask teens who seem impatient how long they are
willing to wait and giving them a realistic time estimate.

Personal and Recreational Questions

Personal or recreational questions is the second largest category
of questions asked by teens in our services and comprises about
15–20% of questions asked. Like homework questions, this category encompasses a seemingly infinite number of topics. Teens
may seek help finding an after-school job or volunteer opportunity, developing a skill, or getting information about a hobby.
Here are some sample questions in this category:

Is it possible that there is a website that I can read a comic book from?

Can you help me find contact addresses for Cuba Gooding Jr. and Clay Aiken?

I DESPERATELY NEED HILARY DUFF'S ADDRESS !!

hi can you tell me the deal with Pinoccho 3000

Can you find me a cool buddy icon site?

im 13 and looking for a paying job

Librarians unaccustomed to working with teenagers may be surprised by the type of questions they ask and sometimes consider them trivial. However, it is wise to remember that the question may be very important to the person who is asking it. As in traditional reference, chat reference librarians should assist users to find the information they need without making value judgments. This can sometimes be difficult online because of the anonymous nature of the interaction, which makes it particularly vulnerable to pranks and abusive behavior.

Inappropriate and Prank Questions

At times, teens and other users approach chat reference services with questions that may appear inappropriate. Peter Bromberg and Marianne Sweet (2004) reviewed 509 chat transcripts (one week's worth) to determine the extent of inappropriate use of QandA NJ. They described two types of inappropriate use: (1) what they termed "goofing around" and (2) "inappropriate language." They found instances of these two categories in only 1.8% of transcripts: goofing around was present in 1.4% of transcripts and .04% of transcripts contained inappropriate language.

Although incidents of inappropriate use are infrequent, they can be memorable and upsetting to reference staff. A common question in chat reference services is about sex. In the following example, a teen is seeking information about this subject.

Teenager: Hello?
Librarian: Welcome to (virtual reference service).
Librarian: Hi (teenager's name). Do you have a question?
Teenager: what is sex?

Librarian: (Teenager's name), This is a library information
      service. Is this research you are doing on sex?
Teenager: yes
Teenager: it is a sex ed class
Librarian: Which grade?
Teenager: 9th
Librarian: Okay. I am looking. by the way, anything in par-
      ticular you would like to know?
Teenager: no
Librarian: Still looking...
Librarian: Sending a page designed for 14-16 year olds.
Librarian: Let me know if this is helpful.
Librarian: http://www.mindbodysoul.gov.uk/sexual/sex-
      menu.html
Teenager: http://www.mindbodysoul.gov.uk/sexual/
      doing_it.html
[Teenager—has disconnected]

In this example, the librarian treated the question as if it
were a serious request for information, rather than a prank, by
doing a reference interview to narrow down the information
need and sending an age-appropriate Web site on sexual development. Once this was done, the student disconnected, so there
is no way to determine whether the question was serious or an
example of goofing around. But the fact that the librarian was
able to provide a reliable source in a helpful manner might
serve as an encouragement for the student to return to the service in the future with less questionable information needs. If
the student were attempting a prank, he or she did not get far
and might be less likely to prank the service again. It is possible
that most questions of a sexual nature are likely to be pranks,
but this is only discerned after a thorough reference interview.
Issues of sexuality are often very important to teens so a question that appears to be about sex is not always an attempt to rile
the librarian.

There are other instances of inappropriate use, including
what Bromberg and Sweet (2004) labeled the "goofing around"
category. For example, at times, teenagers attempt to use the
chat reference service as a chat room. The transcript below is an
example of a teen's using the service because he or she is bored:

Teenager: hello
Librarian: hello.
Teenager: hello (librarian's name)
Librarian: Good morning, (teenager's name). How can I
    help you today?
Teenager: how are you today?
Librarian: Fine, how are you?
Teenager: well i'm just board
Librarian: Bored with your homework questions?
Teenager: how did you know?
Librarian: Here's something fun and interesting, from the
    CBC
Librarian: (page sent)
Teenager: what do you do on it?
Librarian: It just has some games and such.
Teenager: thank you!!!BUNCHES!

In this instance, the online librarian turned the "chat" session into an opportunity to provide a resource for the bored teenager. We believe that when teens access online library services, librarians should seize the opportunity to provide them with excellent service and quality sources, whether or not they are approaching the service in a serious manner. Some teens may not understand the purpose and rules of chat reference services, and it is beneficial to both librarians and users if librarians approach them in a spirit of helpfulness and collaboration. By doing so, librarians can take advantage of an opportunity to promote the service and by extension, their physical libraries. When teens ask what some consider inappropriate questions, we recommend that librarians take these questions seriously and attempt to transform them into reference transactions. If the teen persists in asking inappropriate questions or uses foul or abusive language, the librarian always has the option of disconnecting. Librarians often forget that they can control when the session ends in the chat reference environment.

In addition to these specific techniques, many chat reference services provide online reference staff with scripted messages that can be sent when the service is not being used appropriately. These scripts provide support to the librarians by offering quick and neutral responses to rude and inappropriate behavior. Some examples of scripted messages are:

"I am happy to help you find information about—but I am not allowed to give advice".

"Your language is inappropriate. Please change it, or you will be disconnected."

"This is a library information service. When you have a reference question, we will be glad to help you. Goodbye."

Crisis Questions

The fourth category of adolescent use of chat reference is teens in crisis—"cry-for-help" questions. Although crisis questions are rare, they are often memorable because they are stressful. Librarians feel a natural urge to help but are prevented from doing so because the teen in crisis is not physically present. Also, teen questions about suicide, eating disorders, self-mutilation, and other such topics invariably raise the question of legitimacy: is the question for real or is it a prank? Does the teen need the information for personal reasons or for a paper? Reference librarians handle these questions as they would in the library, by providing referrals to hotlines, crisis counseling services, and organizations that may be of assistance. Although librarians are not responsible for counseling teenagers, addressing emotional content may be helpful in online interactions (Radford and Thompson, 2004). Sometimes, just acknowledging emotional content in a chat session, without actually getting into detail, can pave the way for a more productive and satisfying session.

Summary of Question Categories

The four categories we have created are very broad and could be broken down into a large number of subtypes. Chat reference services might consider sampling methods to study the types of questions they are receiving and to ascertain best practices for answering these. Each type of question can pose challenges to librarians. Homework questions can involve complex information needs by students who are unprepared to do the level of work required; personal questions may border on requests for advice; inappropriate questions can be stressful and frustrating to librarians, who often feel the urge to lecture rude students; and cries for help can be heart-breaking. Because online sessions with teens pose numerous challenges to librarians, it can sometimes be helpful to consult with experts who are knowledgeable about teen behavior.

TIPS FOR WORKING WITH TEENS

In May 2004, after librarians expressed frustration with rude and inappropriate teen online behavior, the coordinator of Colorado's statewide reference service approached the Colorado Young Adult Advocates in Libraries committee and asked them to meet with a group of librarians who staff the service. The group met to review transcripts and to discuss effective strategies for communicating with teens in the chat reference environment. The following recommendations are a result of those discussions:

- At the beginning of the session, send a short, friendly message to build rapport. This lets them know they are chatting with a real person. Long scripted messages seem automated.
- Send chat updates and input regularly.
- Students need to build trust with the librarian and the service. This often develops over time and requires several sessions. Teens may want to test the service and need some time and space to explore. Sometimes this testing can take the form of pranks or goofing around.
- When conducting the reference interview, ask specific questions. Teens don't always know how to formulate their questions or narrow their subjects.
- Provide bibliographic instruction and information literacy at a level they can handle. Younger teens may feel overwhelmed more quickly than older teens. Attempt to discover what grade they are in by asking and then adjust your instruction appropriately.
- Suggest library materials and scientific Web sites such as *Gray's Anatomy* to answer questions that might be pranks, but keep in mind that sexual questions are not always pranks.

- Draw the line early. Let students know what is unacceptable and what you need from them.
- If they are impatient, suggest they come back again when they have more time.

CONCLUSION

Anecdotal evidence suggests that teens are using chat reference services in large numbers. While we have been able to obtain usage statistics from several services, it would be helpful to conduct a nationwide survey to determine teen use of these services. If teens become accustomed to using these services for high school research, they may continue to use them during their college years. Research on teen use of technology and the Internet and how it affects their development is increasing in other fields, but practitioners and researchers in the library and information science have yet to address the issues that teens using their services present. Future studies might examine question types in a more detailed and systematic manner. In addition, librarians might use the data they are gathering in order to partner with educators to meet student needs. While we have touched on many issues in a cursory manner, we hope our overview of teen use of chat reference services will serve to inspire further empirical, theoretical, and practical inquiries into this topic. Continued teen use of chat reference services may be critical to the survival and future funding of these services.

REFERENCES

Abram, Stephen, and Judy Luther. 2004. "Born with the Chip." *Library Journal* 129, no. 8 (May 1, 2004): 34-37. Available at: www.libraryjournal.com/article/CA411572 (accessed September 9, 2005).

AskColorado Collaborative Virtual Reference. 2004. "Advice on Working with Teens," www.aclin.org/reference/advice.html (accessed September 9, 2005).

AskColorado Collaborative Virtual Reference. 2005. *Usage Statistics*, www.aclin.org/reference/stats.html (accessed September 9, 2005).

Boneva, Bonka S., Amy Quinn, Robert E. Kraut, Sara Kiesler, Irina Shklovski. (In press). "Teenage Communication in the Instant Messaging Era." In *Domesticating Information Technology*, edited by R. Kraut, M. Brynin, and S. Kiesler. New York: Oxford University Press, http//:homenet.hcii.cs.cmu.edu/progress/research.html (accessed September 9, 2005).

Bromberg, Peter. "[DIG_REF] Addressing Pranks." Online posting. July 27, 2004. DIG_REF, www.vrd.org/Dig_Ref/dig_ref.shtml> (accessed September 9, 2005).

Coffman, Steve, and Linda Arrett. 2004. "To Chat or Not to Chat—Taking Another Look at Virtual Reference, Part 1." *Searcher* 12, no. 7 (July/August), www.infotoday.com/searcher/jul04/arret_coffman.shtm (accessed September 9, 2005).

Csikszentmihalyi, Mihaly, and Reed Larson. 1984. *Being Adolescent: Conflict and Growth in the Teenage Years*. New York: Basic Books.

Giedd Jay N., John W. Snell, Nicholas Lange, Jagath C. Rajapakse, B.J. Casey, Debra Kaysen, Catherine A. Vaituzis, Yolanda C. Vauss, Susan D. Hamburger, Patricia L. Kozuch, Judith L. Rapoport. 1996. Quantitative Magnetic Resonance Imaging of Human Brain Development: Ages 4–18. *Cerebral Cortex* 6, no. 4: 551–560.

Greene, Louise W., and Joseph Thompson. 2004. Teen Encounters with Virtual Reference Services Focus Group. Unpublished raw data. [Focus Group Transcript].

Greenfield, Patricia Marks, and Kaveri Subrahmanyam. 2003. Online Discourse in a Teen Chatroom: New Codes and New Modes of Coherence in a Visual Medium. *Applied Developmental Psychology* 24, no. 6 (December): 713–738.

Lance, Keith, and Don Dickerson. 2005. "AskColorado's First Year Online." Fast Facts: Recent Statistics from the Library Research Service, Ed3/110.10/No. 223 (March 28), www.lrs.org/documents/fastfacts/223_AskColorado.pdf (accessed September 9, 2005).

Maczewski, Mechthild. 2002. "Exploring identities through the Internet: Youth experiences online." *Child and Youth Care Forum* 31, no. 2 (April): 111–129.

Mariner, Vince. "RE: [DIG_REF] Teen Use of Virtual Reference." E-mail to Sharon Morris. Personal Correspondence Oct. 12, 2004.

Massey-Burzio, Virginia. 1998. "From the Other Side of the Reference Desk: A Focus Group Study at Johns Hopkins University." *The Journal of Academic Librarianship* 24, no. 3: 208–215.

Merchant, Guy. 2001. "Teenagers in Cyberspace: An Investigation of Language Use and Language Change in Internet Chatrooms." *Journal of Research in Reading* 24, no. 3: 293–306.

National Institutes of Mental Health. Division of Intramural Research and Programs. 2004. NIMH Child Branch Research Articles, http://intramural.nimh.nih.gov/chp/articles/index.html (accessed September 9, 2005).

National Telecommunications and Information Administration. 2002. *A Nation Online: How Americans Are Expanding Their Use of the Internet*, www.ntia.doc.gov/ntiahome/dn/html/anationonline.htm (accessed September 9, 2005).

PBS Frontline. 2002. *Inside the Teenage Brain*, www.pbs.org/wgbh/pages/frontline/shows/teenbrain/ (accessed September 9, 2005).

The Pew Internet and American Life Project. 2001. *Teenage Life Online: The Rise of the Instant-Message Generation and the Impact on Friendships and Family Relationships*, www.pewinternet.org/pdfs/PIP_Teens_Report.pdf (accessed September 9, 2005).

Radford, Marie, and Joseph Thompson. 2004. "Hmmm . . . Just a Moment While I Keep Looking": Interpersonal Communication in Chat Reference. Presentation at the Tenth Annual Reference Research Forum. American Library Association Annual Conference (June 27), Orlando, Florida.

Simpson, A. Rae. 2001. *Raising Teens: A Synthesis of Research and a Foundation for Action*. Boston: Center for Health Communication, Harvard School of Public Health.

Steinberg, Laurence. 1998. "Adolescence." In *The Gale Encyclopedia of Childhood and Adolescence*, edited by Jerome Kagan (pp. 10–14). Detroit: Gale Research.

Strauch, Barbara. 2003. *The Primal Teen: What the New Discoveries about the Teenage Brain Tell Us About Our Kids*. New York: Doubleday.

Subrahmanyam, Kaveri, Patricia Greenfield, Robert Kraut, and Elisheva Gross. 2001. "The Impact of Computer Use on Children's and Adolescents' Development. *Applied Developmental Psychology* 22, no. 1 (January-February): 7–30.

Subrahmanyam, Kaveri, Patricia Greenfield, and Brendesha Tynes. 2004. "Constructing Sexuality and Identity in an Online Teen Chat Room." *Applied Developmental Psychology* 25, no. 6 (November-December): 651–666.

Tynes, Brendesha, Lindsey Reynolds, and Patricia M. Greenfield. 2004. "Adolescence, Race, and Ethnicity on the Internet: A Comparison of Discourse in Monitored vs. Unmonitored Chat Rooms." *Applied Developmental Psychology* 25, no. 6 (November-December): 667-684.

UCLA Internet Report. 2003. *Surveying the Digital Future: Year Three*, www.ccp.ucla.edu/pdf/UCLA-Internet-Report-Year-Three.pdf (accessed September 9, 2005).

U.S. Census Bureau. 2000. QT-P2. *Single Years of Age under 30 Years and Sex: 2000*. Census 2000 Summary File 1, Matrix PCT12, http://factfinder.census.gov/servlet/SAFFPeople?-sse (accessed September 9, 2005).

Wolak, Janis, Kimberly J. Mitchell, David Finkelhor. 2003. "Escaping or Connecting? Characteristics of Youth Who Form Close Online Relationships." *Journal of Adolescence* 26, no. 1 (February): 105–119.

Young Adult Library Services Association (YALSA). Professional Development Center. 2003. *Young Adults Deserve the Best: Competencies for Librarians Serving Youth*, www.ala.org/ala/yalsa/profdev/yacompetencies/competencies.htm (accessed September 8, 2005).

Chapter 2

Investigating Interpersonal Communication in Chat Reference: Dealing with Impatient Users and Rude Encounters[1]

Marie L. Radford

OVERVIEW

Chat reference services have emerged as vital alternatives to the traditional face-to-face reference encounter. This study explores the quality of the interpersonal aspects of chat that have been shown to be critical to successful face-to-face reference interactions. A total of 245 randomly selected chat transcripts from a statewide chat reference service (Maryland AskUsNow!)[2] were qualitatively analyzed. Analysis consisted of careful reading and coding, utilizing and refining the category scheme developed from a pilot study of 44 transcripts. The theoretical framework of Watzlawick, Beavin, and Jackson (1967) was applied, differentiating between content aspects of information exchange, and relational (affect) aspects. Results confirm pilot study findings that a wide range of interpersonal skills important to face-to-face reference success is present (although modified) in chat environments. Positive behaviors facilitating open communication, as well as negative behaviors that pose barriers were identified. Behaviors of rude or impatient users are identified and discussed. Recommendations for practitioners are suggested.

INTRODUCTION

Research in Virtual Reference Service (VRS) evaluation is in its early stages, with many reports focusing on questions of accuracy and efficiency or describing individual services and clients (Kasowitz, Bennett, and Lankes, 2000). However, this paper takes a different approach and is among the first to apply communication theory to an exploration of these relational (socioemotional) aspects of chat reference. Analysis resulted in the refinement of the pilot study findings reported at the Virtual Reference Desk conference in 2003 (Radford, 2003), greatly enlarging the preliminary category scheme that identified interpersonal dimensions that facilitated or were barriers to communication.

Library resources and accompanying services have undergone rapid transformation since the introduction of the Web in 1993 and the debut of asynchronous reference services (i.e., e-mail) and, beginning in 1999, synchronous services (i.e., chat reference or Ask a Librarian). Virtual reference services (VRS) gradually have become features of a large number of public and academic library homepages (Johnson, 2004). Since access to electronic information through library Web pages is now commonplace, librarians have recognized the importance of providing digital reference assistance on the user's desktop. Reference assistance is now offered in numerous formats, and library clients turn to Web-based services because they are convenient and often operate during hours that the physical library is not open (Ruppel and Fagan, 2002). Research on traditional face-to-face (FtF) reference interactions has shown that interpersonal aspects are critical to client's assessments of success (Radford, 1993, 1999; Dewdney and Ross, 1994). However, it is not yet known whether these findings can be generalized to virtual reference environments. Several scholars have noted that there is a lack of research in this area and recommend more empirical study, especially research integrating client perspectives (e.g., Kasowitz, Bennett and Lankes, 2000; McClure and Lankes, 2001; Nilsen, 2004; Novotny, 2001; Ronan, 2003; Whitlatch, 2001). In addition, Ruppel and Fagan (2002) call for more qualitative study and analysis of chat reference conversations.

VRS encounters provide an interesting and unique context for study for numerous reasons, including the fact that these encounters produce a complete transcript of the session. VRS transcripts not only capture the complete text of conversations and records of the Web resources that were pushed to the client, but also, in some systems, time stamps for each response. Content analyses that were previously difficult and obtrusive in FtF encounters are made possible by the existence of the transcripts.

LITERATURE REVIEW

Library and Information Science (LIS) Literature

There is a large body of LIS research that studies the content (task, information exchange) aspects of FtF reference encounters (see Baker & Lancaster, 1991). During the 1990s a growing number of studies were conducted on the interpersonal dimensions of FtF reference in a variety of library contexts, such as school (e.g., Chelton, 1997, 1999), public (e.g., Dewdney and Ross 1994, Ross and Dewdney, 1998), and academic libraries (e.g., Radford, 1993, 1998, 1999). In 1996, the Reference and User Services Association (RUSA) of the American Library Association issued "Guidelines for Behavioral Performance of Reference and Information Services Professionals" (RUSA, 2004). These guidelines covered such interpersonal aspects as approachability, listening and demonstrating interest in the user's question, and involving the user in the search for information. The guidelines have been recently updated to include recommendations for behavior in virtual reference encounters, signaling a greater awareness since 1996 of the need to pay attention to relational, interpersonal aspects of reference work in addition to the need to provide correct information to the client (RUSA, 2004).

According to Sloan (2004), literature on VRS is rapidly proliferating, but many services are only beginning to conduct studies of user behavior, with evaluation of academic library service far outnumbering studies of the public libraries (Nilsen, 2004) or studies of statewide services. Evaluations of efficiency and effectiveness in task dimensions, such as correctly answering the questions posed, are appearing in the literature in increasing numbers (e.g., see Carter and Janes, 2002; Foley, 2002; Gross and McClure, 2001a, 2001b; Kaske and Arnold, 2002; and White, Abels, and Kaske, 2003). However, few research studies have appeared on the relational dimensions of virtual reference. Among those that do are Carter and Janes (2002), Janes and Mon (2004), Nilsen (2004), Radford (2003), and Ruppel and Fagan (2002). Carter and Janes (2002) analyzed over 3,000 e-mail transcripts from the Internet Public Library (IPL, http://www.ipl.org) and found that unsolicited "thank-you" messages were received for 19.7% of the interactions. Janes and Mon (2004) performed a follow-up study of 810 IPL e-mail reference transcripts and found a 15.9% thank-you rate. These researchers contend that this rate is an indicator of quality service from the user's point of view.

Ruppel and Fagan (2002) compared clients' perceptions of virtual reference service and the traditional reference desk in a study of the use of an instant messaging (IM) chat reference service. They concluded: "New library services generally succeed when the 'best' aspects of traditional services are incorporated. Transferring effective reference behaviors from the traditional desk environment to the IM service is challenging, given the absence of facial expressions and body language" (p. 9).

Nilsen (2004) reported on 42 MLS students' perceptions of VRS encounters. Results indicated that relational factors are important to the clients, and Nilsen concludes that "simply answering user queries is not enough. User satisfaction with reference services depends on consistent use of best reference behavior" (p. 16). The present study extends the work described above and reports one of the first evaluations of transcripts randomly selected from a statewide VRS.

Radford (2003)[3] analyzed 44 transcripts submitted for consideration for the Library Systems and Services, LLC Samuel Swett Green Award. Radford found that interpersonal aspects important to FtF reference success are present (although modified) in the chat environment. These include: techniques for rapport building, compensation for lack of nonverbal cues, strategies for relationship development, evidence of deference and respect, face-saving tactics, greeting rituals, and closing rituals. She identified interpersonal facilitators as well as barriers to success.

Communication Literature

There is a substantial body of research on relational aspects of virtual communication environments in the computer-mediated communication (CMC) literature. Walther and D'Addario (2001: 325) note that CMC "encompasses both impersonal, task-focused activities as well as relational development and maintenance activities." Exemplified by a seminal article (Rice and Love, 1987), there have been a number of research projects that have focused upon the relational, or "socioemotional" content in electronic communication. In their study of computer conferencing, Rice and Love defined "socioemotional content" as "interactions that show solidarity, tension relief, agreement, antagonism, tension, and disagreement" (1987: 93) in contrast to "task-dimensional content," which is defined as "interactions that ask for or give information or opinion." They challenged a basic assumption that CMC dialogue "transmit less of the natural richness and interaction of interpersonal communication than face-to-face interaction" (Rice and Love, 1987: 87). They found that 30% of the sentences sent had socioemotional content, and their results suggest that more active and more experienced users tended to send more messages of this type.

Other researchers have also found that users in CMC environments increasingly adapt their relational, socioemotional behavior (through use of emoticons, punctuation, all capital letters, etc.) to compensate for the lack of nonverbal cues (see Carter, 2003; Rezabek and Cochenour, 1998; Walther, 1992, 1994; Walther and D'Addario, 2001). Danet, Ruedenberg-Wright, and Rosenbaum-Tamari (1997) noted that CMC was becoming more playful than serious. This trend has continued to grow as more and more people have come to use e-mail and instant messaging (IM) on a daily basis, which was estimated to be 174 million people in 2003 (Metz, Clyman and Todd, 2003: 128). It is especially notable in the communication of adolescents who use IM as the preferred mode for social messaging rather than task-related messaging (Metz, Clyman, and Todd, 2003). The impact of IM use on library VRS dialogue is clearly evident in the results of this study and is expected to continue to grow.

THEORETICAL PERSPECTIVE AND RESEARCH QUESTIONS

According to Watzlawick, Beavin, and Jackson's seminal work *Pragmatics of Human Communication* (1967); all messages have both a content (task) and relational dimension. This theoretical framework differentiates between the content aspects of information exchange and the relational (affect, interpersonal) aspects. Watzlawick, Beavin, and Jackson's framework has formed the basis of numerous empirical studies, including investigations of FtF reference interactions in academic libraries (Radford, 1999, 1996, 1993). The present research applies this approach to a new context: virtual reference dialogs. The theoretical framework of Watzlawick, Beavin and Jackson (1967) and the above literature review have led to the following research questions:

1. What relational dimensions are present in chat reference transcripts?
2. Are there differences in the relational dimensions and patterns of chat clients and librarians? If so, what are they?
3. How do clients and librarians compensate for lack of nonverbal cues in chat reference?
4. What is the relationship between content and relational dimensions in determining the quality of chat reference encounters?

METHODOLOGY

The sample of 245 transcripts was selected using the software vendor 24/7 Reference's "Reports" feature to capture the transcripts of every Maryland AskUsNow! session recorded from November 2003 to February 2004, a population of 12,029 sessions.

From this population, a random sample of 245 useable sessions was selected.

Participants included Maryland librarians and others working throughout the national 24/7 Reference cooperative and their VR clients. To protect the participant's privacy, each transcript was stripped of any identifying features prior to analysis, including the client's name, e-mail address, and IP address, and the librarian's identifying initials, name, and library location.

The transcripts underwent in-depth qualitative analysis, using and further refining the category scheme developed by Radford (2003) and identifying new categories, especially in the area of barriers. Phi coefficients for intercoder reliability, based upon a random sample of 20% of the transcripts analyzed by two additional trained coders, were .96 and .93, with discussion and adjustments made to resolve areas of disagreement.

Results

The Maryland AskUs Now! study results confirmed the findings of the Green Award study (Radford, 2003) and further developed the category schemes. Since the Maryland data was obtained through random selection, rather than self-selection, the category schemes for relational barriers for both librarians and clients are much more developed than that of the Green Award Study.

Major Themes—Relational Facilitators and Relational Barriers

For both librarians and clients two major themes were found: relational facilitators and relational barriers (see also Radford, 2003, 1999, 1993). Relational facilitators are defined as interpersonal aspects that have a positive impact on the librarian-client interaction and that enhance communication (see also Radford, 1993, 1999). Within facilitators, five subthemes were found to be present for both librarians and clients (although found in different order by percentage of instances): rapport building, deference, compensation for lack of nonverbal cues, greeting ritual, and closing ritual.

Barriers are defined as relational aspects that have a negative impact on the librarian-client interaction and that impede communication (see also Radford, 2003, 1999, 1993). Within barriers there were two subthemes for librarians and clients: closing problems and relational disconnect/failure to build rapport. Table 2-1 is a portion of the larger category scheme that reports the frequency of occurrences for the client relational barriers.[4]

Closing Problems Subtheme

Closing problems is a large category, present in 95 out of 245 transcripts (39%). Closing problems occur when the chat session is ended abruptly before the librarian and/or user is ready to end. It is difficult to determine the cause of these problems because transcripts do not indicate reasons for the disconnection. Some abrupt departures may be caused by technical glitches, other times the user may decide to sign off quickly for unknown reasons, sometimes referred to as the "disappearing user." Many times the librarians continue to push Web sites to the clients in the hope that the client will receive the full transcript even after the disconnect. In the example shown in Table 2-2, the client makes an abrupt closing. Reading the transcripts, it is impossible to determine what happened to cause this closing. It is possible that the client is engrossed in reviewing the Web site

Table 2-1
Client Relational Barriers (N=245)

CB 1 Closing problems—Signing off abruptly (95, 39%)

CB 2 Relational Disconnect/Failure to Build Rapport (35, 14%)
1. Impatience (24, 10%)
2. Poor attitude/rude/insulting/FLAMING (10, 4%)
3. Disconfirming (e.g., I already have that information) (7, 3%)
4. Use of profanity or inappropriate language (5 - 2%)
5. Failure/refusal to provide information when asked (4, 2%)
6. Derisive use of spelling out nonverbal behaviors (2, 1%)
7. Mistakes/Misunderstandings (e.g., user types wrong word, provides wrong information) (2, 1%)

Each number in parenthesis is the number of transcripts that exhibited the category. Numbers below the main categories (in bold) do not total since transcripts can exhibit more than one subcategory. Percentages are rounded to the nearest whole number.

Table 2-2
Example of Closing Problems Subtheme of Barriers

Abrupt Closing—Client (108062)

> Client: information on streptococcus mutans
>
> [A librarian will be with you in about a minute.]
>
> [Librarian (name)—A librarian has joined the session.]
>
> Librarian: Hi, (client's name). What kind of information do you need about this?
> Client: how does streptococcus mutans attack?
> Librarian: Let me look and see if I can find some information.
> Client: ok
> Librarian: Customer, I found a website from a dental college that seems to explain this issue. I'm going to send you the link in just a second. . .
>
> [Item sent] http://www.ncl.ac.uk/dental/oralbiol/oralenv/tutorials/mutans.htm
>
> Librarian: Can I help you with anything else?
> Librarian: Customer, are you still there? Can I help you with anything else?
>
> [A transcript of this session will be e-mailed to you after we disconnect—it will contain the text of our chat and links to all of the websites we visited.]
>
> [Thank you for using Maryland AskUsNow! If you have any further questions, please contact us again.]
>
> Note: Text in square brackets is system generated or is a pre-written script selected and sent by the librarian.

<end>

Note: These transcripts are verbatim and contain the original grammar and spelling.

that the librarian sent, or had to leave their computer suddenly for unknown reasons.

Relational Disconnect/Failure to Build Rapport Subtheme

Transcripts with statements in the Relational Disconnect/Failure to Build Rapport category were 35 (14%) out of 245 transcripts.

Evidence of impatience (e.g., client typing "hurry up!") was found in 24 (10%) of the transcripts. Demonstrations of a poor attitude, rudeness, flaming, or insults on the part of clients were only found in 10 (4%) of the transcripts, a relatively low number.

In a study of FtF interactions, Radford (1999) defined rapport building as behavior that "involves conversation encouraging give and take, establishment of mutual understanding, and development of relationships" (p. 25). Relational Disconnect/Failure to Build Rapport is defined as behavior that discourages give and take, mutual understanding, and development of relationships.

Table 2-3 provides an example of the Relational Disconnect/Failure to Build Rapport Subtheme that demonstrates multiple categories of negative behaviors: impatient, poor attitude (rude, insulting, flaming), and derisive use of spelling out of nonverbal behaviors. This client, self-disclosed to be in sixth grade, is seeking information on goldfish, and begins with a polite manner, but soon reveals impatience by telling the librarian to hurry up: "okay please hury it up thanks." The librarian is trying to help the client quickly, but when a Web site on fish instead of goldfish is sent, the client becomes more impatient and capitalizes the word FISH resulting in a flame. The librarian responds to the flame by giving the client a reprimand in the next line: "You don't need to capitalize." The client replies to this reprimand with a longer and now insulting flame "I ONLY WANT GOLDFISH INFO GET THAT THROUGH YOUR THICK HEAD!" Then the client exits with a stream of abuse that includes name-calling and derision of the librarian's professional and personal life: "get a real job loser I bet your spouse is cheating on you! hahaha!" The librarian quickly moves to end the interaction by pushing a goodbye script, asking the user to return when he or she can be more patient.

This interaction exemplifies how emotional content can have a negative impact on the success of an interaction. In this case, the librarian's reprimand had the opposite effect of what was intended. Instead of becoming less rude, the reprimand provoked more rude behavior from the client.

Table 2-4 demonstrates the subcategory "Disconfirming," defined as behaviors that are critical of, contradictory, show

Table 2-3
Example of Relational Disconnect/Failure to Build Rapport Subtheme

Poor Attitude (impatient, rude, insulting, flaming)—Client (000008)

Client: goldfish info

Librarian: [A librarian will be with you in about 2 minutes.]

[Librarian (name)—A librarian has joined the session.]

Librarian: [Welcome to Maryland AskUsNow! I'm looking at your question right now; it will be just a moment.]
Librarian: What kind of information do you need about goldfish?
Client: okay
Client: I want to do alittle research for a school science fair project
Librarian: So you want to do a project with goldfish?
Client: please don't send me things for science project ideas
Client: thank you
Librarian: So what research do you need? There's lots of information about goldfish
Client: i want to know everythingaboutfish and thier breathing rates with temperature
Librarian: OK, let me take a look
Client: i want things for someone on a sixth grade level too
Librarian: I'll try. I;m looking
Client: okay please hury it up thanks

<text omitted>

Librarian: Yes it is. I do have one page that may help. I'm sending it

[Item sent]

Librarian: Take a look and I'm going to look a little further
Librarian: Here's another possibility. It's not goldfish specifically, but it's about fish
Client: this is not what i'm looking for I want info on...........FISH!

[Item sent]

Librarian: You don't need to capitalize. Did you read the last paragraph?
Client: I ONLY WANT GOLDFISH INFO GET THAT THROUGH YOUR THICK HEAD!
Client: what is in the last paragraph?
Librarian: [If you need further assistance and can be more patient, please feel free to contact us again. Thank you for using Maryland AskUsNow! Goodbye!]
Client: geta real job loser I bet your spose is cheatingon you! hahaha!

Table 2-4
Example of Relational Disconnect/Failure to Build Rapport Subtheme

Disconfirming—Client and Librarian (138669)

> Client: I have some word puzzles I need help with
>
> Librarian: [A librarian will be with you in about a minute.]
>
> [hpl- XXX - A librarian has joined the session.]
>
> Librarian: [Hello, this is the reference librarian. I'm reading your question...]
> Librarian: Such as?
> Client: the puzzle gives you a clue like 12=M in a Y
> Client: the answer would be 12 monthe in a year
> Librarian: Does this involve calculus?
> Client: no
> Client: M stands fo Months and Y stand fo Year
> Client: there is no math involved
> Librarian: I have no idea what that is. Would it not be better to go to your local library and show that to a librarian?

<text omitted>

> Librarian: I think that it is too obvious. Just fill in the blanks with the words that make sense.

<text omitted>

> Client: an I give some of the ones I don't have yet?
> Librarian: Go ahead.
> Client: can you help me solve them
> Librarian: Go ahead.
> Librarian: Yes, I will help you.
> Client: 40 T and AB

<text omitted>

> Librarian: Aladin and the 40 thieves.
> Client: 12 R in a BM
> Librarian: This must be in reference to something you have to read. I don't have any idea what they are

<text omitted>

> Librarian: Why don't you call some of your classmates to see what they are doing about this.
> Client: I have called all the people I can and they are working on the some ones I am
> Client: we are sharing answeres as we get them

(Continued)

Table 2-4
Example of Relational Disconnect/Failure to Build
Rapport Subtheme (*Continued*)

Client: do you have any Idea were I can get answers to this word
  puzzle??????
Librarian: Let me see if there's a website.
Client: THANK YOU
Librarian: I will send you a couple of sites.
Client: thanks

[Item sent] http://www.thepotters.com/puzzles.html

Client: those are word searches
Librarian: This is all I can find. For more please go to your public library.
Librarian: At this time I must attend to other customers. If you need more
  help, please contact us again. Goodbye, and thank you for using the
  Maryland AskUsNow! service.
Client: [y]ou didn't help me very much

<end>

indifference, or disqualify (speak for) the other (see Mathews, 1983). Here, the librarian is disconfirming to the client (self-disclosed in omitted text to be in seventh grade) and the client is disconfirming to the librarian. At first, the librarian reassures the client that she or he will help with a homework assignment on word puzzles. The librarian seems stumped by the question, although says that the answers are "obvious," which is disconfirming to the client, implying that "obvious" answers should not need the assistance of a librarian. The librarian then says that the answers should be in assigned readings, tries to refer the client to fellow students and then to the public library, negative closure strategies found by Ross and Dewdney (1998) in FtF interactions. Later, the librarian pushes an inappropriate Web site, but the client points out that "those are word searches," disconfirming the librarian by implying incompetence in judging the site's usefulness. The librarian gives a disclaimer that no more could be found and pushes a goodbye script, abruptly ending the interaction. The client responds to the robotic script with the wistful and dejected comment, "[y]ou didn't help me very much." The client had been reassured by the librarian that "Yes, I will help you," but, in the end, help was not forthcoming and the client is obviously not satisfied by the referrals to class-mates or to the public library. The librarian appeared frustrated and pushed the page on word searches perhaps in the hope that it would be helpful (or perhaps to see if it would appease).

Table 2-5 demonstrates the subcategory "Mistakes/Misun-derstandings," defined as unintentionally providing misinfor-mation or instances of accidental misunderstandings. In this example, the client (self-disclosed to be the parent of a 15-year-old) has a multipart question and makes a one key-stroke error in typing "diving classes" for the intended topic, "driving classes." The librarian, a self-disclosed diving enthusiast, starts searching for "diving" without any probe questions on any of the multiple parts of the question. This type of error is quickly rectified, once the client realizes the mistake. The client corrects the librarian in a manner that is not gentle and is disconfirming to the librarian, and neither apologizes or admits making the mistake.

Table 2-5
Example of Relational Disconnect/Failure to Build Rapport Subtheme

---

Mistakes/Misunderstandings—Client (000013)

   Client: Hello. I need help findind information on the following: where in baltimore, maryland can I find peppermint oil, if a 15 year old can start diving classes now, and can a 15 year old get a office job at this age?

   Librarian: [A librarian will be with you in about a minute.]

   [XXX—A librarian has joined the session.]

   Librarian: One moment please.
   Librarian: I will see what I can find.
   Client: alright
   Librarian: After looking at a few web sites it seems that beginning scuba diving classes start at age 12 to 16. it depends on how good a swimmer the person is. As a scuba diver myself I think the age range sounds right.
   Client: i don't want any scuba diving classes
   Client: i want driving classes

<text omitted>

DISCUSSION AND IMPLICATIONS

As can be seen from the examples in Tables 2-2 through 2-5, these transcripts provide a rich data source; indeed only a small fraction of the data could be shared here. It can be noted that several of the clients who displayed rude or impatient behavior were either self-disclosed to be middle-school students or had the type of questions relating to schoolwork that indicate that they are young adults, although two of the examples above (including the example for abrupt closing) are adults. On the topic of handling a potentially problematic user in traditional encounters, there are several excellent articles on how to understand and approach young adults in a positive manner (e.g., see Bunge, 1994; Chelton, 1997, 1999; Jones, 1996; and Turner, 1993), as well as how to work with difficult adult clients (e.g., see McNeil and Johnson, 1996; Rubin, 2000; Smith, 1993; and Weingand, 1997). Much of the advice offered for problematic FtF encounters can be put to good use in cyberspace. Basic interpersonal conventions, such as manners, use of polite expressions, and being aware of the potential impact of words and attitudes apply, although the lack of nonverbal behaviors, such as a smile, are not there to soften the verbal exchange. This research indicates that VRS clients have quickly adapted to the chat conventions including use of smiley faces (emoticons), alternative/truncated spelling and repeated punctuation to compensate for this lack.

Research Questions

Here, discussion has been threaded throughout the presentation of the results. Attention is now drawn back to the research questions.

Research Question 1: What relational dimensions are present in chat reference transcripts?

The category schemes for both librarians and clients reveal a detailed summary of the wide variety of socioemotional/relational aspects (see Radford and Thompson, 2004b). These findings demonstrate a resonance with other researchers (e.g., Walther and Burgoon, 1992; Walther, 1992; 1993) who have found that computer-mediated communication "is no less personal than FtF"

(Walther, 1996: 33). This paper provided detailed examples of the interpersonal dimensions that are present in client barriers.

Research Question 2: Are there differences in the relational dimensions/patterns of chat clients and librarians?

Transcript analysis indicates both similarities and differences in the patterns of clients and librarians, especially in the area of barriers, where there were more rude or impatient clients, and in the area of closing problems, which were far more numerous for clients. Although clients show more rudeness and impatience, librarians also demonstrate negative behaviors in disconfirming or being condescending, and, at times, in mirroring rude behavior.

Research Question 3: How do clients and librarians compensate for lack of nonverbal cues in chat reference?

Again, analysis showed a rich array of strategies for compensation, with clients showing more informality and willingness to use chat shortcuts, abbreviations, and emoticons (see also Rice and Love, 1987; Ronan, 2003).

Research Question 4: What is the relationship between content and relational dimensions in determining the quality of chat reference encounters?

This research question still remains largely unanswered, although the relationship between relational and content quality can be inferred in some cases (see Table 2-3 in which the reprimand by the librarian prompted a dramatic increase in incivility). It is, however, impossible to have a clear answer to this question without asking the participants.

This research demonstrates the complexity of virtual reference interactions and the value of applying communication theory and constructs to investigations of these encounters. One theoretical implication is that models of VRS must include the relational as well as the content/task dimensions, and this study furthers this work (see also Radford, 1993, 1999). There are many implications for practitioners of chat reference from these results. An important implication is that interpersonal dimensions are present in virtual reference environments and that chat librarians and clients need to be aware and skilled in the basics of interpersonal communication. Practitioners are not only answering questions, they are also building relationships with clients in every virtual reference encounter (see also Radford, 1993, 1999).

Especially in these early days of VRS, librarians are teaching clients, by the way that they respond, how to use the service and also what behaviors are expected. One implication to consider is that the success of VRS may be contingent upon building positive relationships with all clients, as the young adult is soon the college student and then the adult. If positive relationships are not formed at early, impressionable ages, the clients may turn elsewhere for their information needs. To assist practitioners in their encounters with rude or impatient chat clients, recommended guidelines, based on the findings of this research are included in Appendix 2-A.

LIMITATIONS

As noted above, in order to protect the privacy of the clients and librarians, all identifying characteristics were stripped from the transcripts. Although this was necessary, it has resulted in a lack of demographic data. This research project is thus limited to what can be seen and inferred from the transcript discourse without any input from the participants. Also, this research is regarded as exploratory. The random sample was designed to be representative and, as such, generalizable to the Maryland AskUsNow! service, but no generalizations to other chat reference services are claimed.

FUTURE DIRECTIONS

In addition to developing a theoretical approach that integrates relational dimensions, more empirical research is needed as many unanswered or partially answered questions remain. As noted above, Research Question 4 can only be partially answered by looking at transcripts. Future research will involve online surveys, FtF interviews, and focus groups with both librarians and clients to provide more definitive answers regarding the relationship of content and relational dimensions to quality. Another direction for future research is to investigate other virtual reference contexts. Research with transcripts from additional statewide service could be compared with these to see if similar patterns emerge. It would also be fruitful to examine transcripts from university and other VR services to compare results. Similarly, it would be interesting to follow up on a variety of findings, to see, for example, the impact of staff education on interpersonal aspects of chat and to investigate whether incidences of rudeness can be reduced through use of humor, tolerance, and confirming behaviors.

CONCLUSION

Much more research needs to be done to understand and improve the quality of chat encounters. As Ronan (2003: 43) notes: "One of the biggest challenges in providing reference services in real-time is learning to communicate effectively with remote users and to translate the interpersonal skills used at the physical reference desk into the virtual environment." This research demonstrates the value of applying communication theory to the VRS context and gives a sense of the insights that can be gained. Future projects will build on these findings to extend knowledge, improve competence, and enable VRS staff to develop the skills to establish rapport and build positive relationships with clients who at times may be impatient or rude.

NOTES

1. A previous version of this chapter was presented at the 2004 Virtual Reference Desk Conference, Cincinnati, Ohio, November 8–9, 2004 (see Radford and Thompson, 2004a).
2. The researcher thanks Maryland AskUsNow! and Joseph Thompson for permission to analyze these transcripts.
3. The Green Award project was the pilot study for the research reported in this paper. The researcher thanks Steve Coffman and LSSI for permission to analyze the Green Award transcripts.

REFERENCES

Baker, Sharon L., and F. Wilfrid Lancaster. 1991. *The Measurement and Evaluation of Library Services* (2nd ed.). Arlington, VA: Information Resources Press.
Bunge, Charles A. 1994. "Responsive Reference Service: Breaking Down Age Barriers." *School Library Journal* 30, no. 3 (March): 142–145.

Carter, David S., and Joseph Janes. 2002. "Unobtrusive Data Analysis of Digital Reference Questions and Service at the Internet Public Library: An Exploratory Study." *Library Trends* 49, no. 2 (Fall): 251–265.

Carter, K. A. 2003. "Type Me How You Feel: Quasi-Nonverbal Cues in Computer-Mediated Communication." *Etc.* 60, no. 1 (Spring): 29–39.

Chelton, Mary K. 1997. "The 'Overdue Kid': A Face-to-Face Library Service Encounter as Ritual Interaction." *Library and Information Science Research* 19, no. 4 (Fall): 387–399.

Chelton, Mary K. 1999. "Behavior of Librarians in School and Public Libraries with Adolescents: Implications for Practice and LIS Education." *Journal of Education for Library and Information Science* 40, no. 2 (Spring): 99–111.

Danet, Brenda, Lucia Ruedenberg-Wright, and Yehudit Rosenbaum-Tamari. 1997. "'HMMM...WHERE'S THAT SMOKE COMING FROM?' Writing, Play and Performance on Internet Relay Chat." *Journal of Computer-Mediated Communication* 2 no. 4: http//jcmc.indiana.edu/vol2/issue4/danet.html (accessed September 8, 2005).

Dewdney, Patricia, and Catherine S. Ross. 1994. "Flying a Light Aircraft: Reference Service Evaluation from the User's Viewpoint." *RQ* 34, no. 2 (Winter): 217–230.

Foley, Marianne. 2002. "Instant Messaging Reference in an Academic Library: A Case Study." *College and Research Libraries* 63, no. 1: 36–45.

Gross, Melissa, and Charles McClure. 2001a. "Assessing Quality in Digital Reference Services Site Visit Reports." Information Use Management and Policy Institute, Florida State University, Tallahassee, dlis.dos.state.fl.us/bld/Research_Office/VRD.StLibFLRpt.Sept29.doc (accessed September 8, 2005).

Gross, Melissa, and Charles McClure. 2001b. "Assessing Quality in Digital Reference Services: Overview of Key Literature on Digital Reference." Information Use Management and Policy Institute, Florida State University, Tallahassee, dlis.dos.state.fl.us/bld/Research_Office/VRDphaseII.LitReview.doc (accessed September 8, 2005).

Janes, Joseph, and Lorri Mon. 2004. "The Thank You Study: User Satisfaction with Digital Reference." Presented at the Meeting of the Association of Library Science Educators (ALISE) (January 6-9), San Diego, CA.

Johnson, Corey M. 2004. "Online Chat Reference: Survey Results From Affiliates of Two Universities." *RUSQ* 43, no. 3: 237–247.

Jones, Patrick. 1996. Opposites Attract: Young Adults and Libraries. In *Patron Behavior in Libraries: A Handbook of Positive Approaches to Negative Situations*, edited by B. McNeil and D. Johnson (pp. 44–55). Chicago: American Library Association.

Kaske, Neil, and Julie Arnold. 2002. An Unobtrusive Evaluation of Online Real Time Library Reference Services. Presented at the American Library Association, Annual Conference (June 15), Atlanta, GA. www.lib.umd.edu/groups/digref/kaskearnoldunobtrusive.html (accessed September 8, 2005).

Kasowitz, Abby, Blythe Bennett, and R. David Lankes. 2000. "Quality Standards for Digital Reference Consortia." *Reference and User Services Quarterly (RUSQ)* 39, no. 4: 355–363.

Mathews, Anne J. 1983. *Communicate! A Librarian's Guide to Interpersonal Relations.* Chicago: American Library Association.

McClure, Charles R., and R. David Lankes. 2001. "Assessing Quality in Digital Reference Services: A Research Prospectus." Information Institute of Syracuse, http://quartz.syr.edu/quality/Overview.htm

McNeil, Beth, and Denise J. Johnson. 1996. *Patron Behavior in Libraries: A Handbook of Positive Approaches to Negative Situations.* Chicago: American Library Association.

Metz, Cade, John Clyman, and Mark Todd. 2003. "IM Everywhere." *PC Magazine* 22, no. 20 (November 11): 128–136.

Nilsen, Kirsti. 2004. "The Library Visit Study: User Experiences at the Virtual Reference Desk." *Information Research* 9, no. 2: paper 171, InformationR.net/ir/9-2/paper171.html (accessed September 8, 2005).

Novotny, Eric. 2001. "Evaluating Electronic Reference Services: Issues, Approaches and Criteria." *The Reference Librarian* 74, no. 74: 103–120.

Radford, Marie L. 1993. Relational Aspects of Reference Interactions: A Qualitative Investigation of the Perceptions of Users and Librarians in the Academic Library. Unpublished doctoral dissertation, Rutgers, The State University of New Jersey. DAI A54/07, 2368.

Radford, Marie L. 1996. "Communication Theory Applied to the Reference Encounter: An Analysis of Critical Incidents." *Library Quarterly* 66, no. 2 (April): 123–137.

Radford, Marie L. 1998. "Approach or Avoidance? The Role of Nonverbal Communication in the Academic Library User's Decision to Initiate a Reference Encounter." *Library Trends* 46, no. 4 (Spring): 699–717.

Radford, Marie L. 1999. *The Reference Encounter: Interpersonal Communication in the Academic Library.* Chicago: ACRL, A Division of the American Library Association.

Radford, Marie L. 2003. "In synch? Evaluating chat reference transcripts." Presented at the Virtual Reference Desk Fifth Annual Conference (November 17-18), San Antonio, TX. www.vrd2003.org/proceedings/presentation.cfm?PID=231 (accessed September 8, 2005).

Radford, Marie L., and Joseph Thompson. 2004a. "Yo Dude! Y R U Typin So Slow?" Presented at the Virtual Reference Desk Sixth Annual Conference (November 8-9), Cincinnati, OH.

Radford, Marie L., and Josepth Thompson. 2004b. "Yo Dude! Y R U Typin So Slow?" Online Proceedings of the Virtual Reference Desk 6th Annual Conference, Cincinnati , OH, November 8-9, www.vrd2004.org/proceedings/presentation.cfm?PID=325 (accessed September 8, 2005).

Reference and User Services Association (RUSA). 2004. Guidelines for Behavioral Performance of Reference and Information Services Professionals, www.ala.org/ala/rusa/rusaprotools/referenceguide/guidelinesbehavioral.htm (accessed October 19, 2005).

Reference and User Services Association (RUSA). (Winter 1996) 200–3. Guidelines for Behavioral Performance of Reference and Information Services Professionals, www.ala.org/ala/rusa/rusaprotools/referenceguide/guidelinesbehavioral.htm

Rezabek, Landra L., and John J. Cochenour. 1998. "Visual Cues in Computer-Mediated Communication: Supplementing Text with Emoticons." *Journal of Visual Literacy* 18, no. 2: 201–215.

Rice, Ronald E., and Gail Love. 1987. "Electronic Emotion: Socio-Emotional Content in a Computer-Mediated Communication Network." *Communication Research* 14, no. 1 (February): 85–108.

Ronan, Jana. 2003. "The Reference Interview Online." *RUSQ* 43, no. 1: 43–47.

Ross, Catherine S., and Patricia Dewdney. 1998. "Negative Closure: Strategies and Counter-Strategies in the Reference Transaction." *RUSQ* 38, no. 2 (Winter): 151–163.

Rubin, Rhea. 2000. *Defusing the Angry Patron: A How-To-Do-It Manual for Librarians.* New York: Neal-Schuman.

Ruppel, Margie, and Jody Condit Fagan. 2002. "Instant Messaging Reference: Users' Evaluation of Library Chat." *Reference Services Review* 30, no. 3: 183–197. Available at: www.lib.siu.edu/~jfagan/papers/imref.html

Sloan, Bernie. 2004. "Digital Reference Services: Bibliography," http://alexia.lis.uiuc.edu/~b-sloan/digiref.html (accessed September 8, 2005).

Smith, Kitty. 1993. *Serving the Difficult Customer: A How-To-Do-It Manual for Library Staff.* New York: Neal-Schuman.

Turner, Anne M. 1993. *It Comes with the Territory: Handling Problem Situations in Libraries.* Jefferson, NC: McFarland.

Walther, Joseph B. 1992. "Interpersonal Effects in Computer-Mediated Interaction: A Relational Perspective." *Communication Research* 19, no. 1 (August): 52–90.

Walther, Joseph B. 1993. "Impression Development in Computer-Mediated Interaction." *Western Journal of Communication* 57, no. 4 (Fall): 381–398.

Walther, Joseph B. 1994. "Anticipated Ongoing Interaction versus Channel Effects on Relational Communication in Computer-Mediated Interaction." *Human Communication Research* 20, no. 4 (June): 473–501.

Walther, Joseph B. 1996. "Computer-Mediated Communication: Impersonal, Interpersonal and Hyperpersonal Interaction." *Communication Research* 23, no. 1: 3-43.

Walther, Joseph B., and Judee K. Burgoon. 1992. "Relational Communication in Computer-Mediated Interaction." *Human Communication Research* 19, no. 18 (September): 50–88.

Walther, Joseph B., and Kyle P. D'Addario. 2001. "The Impacts of Emoticons on Message Interpretation in Computer-Mediated Communication." *Social Science Computer Review* 19, no. 3 (August): 342–347.

Watzlawick, Paul, Janet Beavin, and Donald D. Jackson. 1967. *Pragmatics of Human Communication.* New York: Norton.

Weingand, Darlene E. 1997. *Customer Service Excellence: A Concise Guide for Librarians.* Chicago: American Library Association.

White, Marilyn Domas, Eileen G. Abels, and Neal Kaske. 2003. "Evaluation of
    Chat Reference Service Quality." *D-Lib Magazine* 9, no. 2 (February): 1–13.
Whitlatch, JoBell. (2001). "Evaluating Reference Services in the Electronic
    Age." *Library Trends* 50, no. 2 (Fall): 207–217.

APPENDIX 2-A

Recommendations for Virtual Reference Encounters with Rude or Impatient Clients

- Remember that you have skills and experience in dealing with rude/impatient people in face-to-face encounters. These skills can be just as effective in virtual encounters.
  - Use your common sense, intuition, and experience to defuse problematic encounters.
- When users are impatient ("Hurry, hurry!"), let them know realistically how long you think that the search for the needed information will take.
  - If you estimate that it will take more than a minute or so, tell them and ask if they are willing to wait (e.g., "I know you are in a hurry, but this search will take about 4 to 5 minutes. Can you wait?")
  - Presenting a realistic estimate of the time needed may prevent abrupt user departures.
  - If they can't wait, apologize and present an alternative (e.g., I'm sorry I can't answer your question quickly, but I can email that answer to you within 2-3 days).
  - During the time users are waiting while you search, check in occasionally and give a quick update like "still searching..." Periodic reassurances will also prevent abrupt departures.
- Do not "mirror" rude behavior; this only provokes more rudeness.
- Be polite and professional at all times.
- Resist the urge to reprimand or admonish users for rude behavior or FLAMING, again this only provokes more rude behavior.
- Avoid jargon or language that will create a barrier or send the message that you are blindly following the rulebook.
- Apologize to the user as appropriate, this does not mean that you are accepting blame.
  - An apology can diffuse potentially rude behavior (e.g., "I'm sorry that you had to wait so long; our service is very busy today" or., "I'm sorry that I can't help with

> your request this time, please visit your local library for that information.").

- If the user complains about library service or another librarian, thank them for bringing their concern to your attention and promise to follow-up.
  - Regard a complaint as a gift, as a way to improve service.
- Do not be condescending to a person with a "simple question." Sometimes parents are helping their children with homework and you may insult them. Treat all users with equal courtesy and respect.
- Realize that rude or impatient users are in the minority, but understand that you will encounter one now and then.
  - Your polite response to them instructs them on how to use the service properly in the future.
- Do not take rude behavior personally. Users may be stressed by deadlines or other life problems and their rudeness and impatience usually has nothing to do with you or your service.

PART II

Creating a Reference Future: Training and Staffing

Chapter 3

Training for Online Virtual Reference: Measuring Effective Techniques

Eileen G. Abels and Malissa Ruffner

OVERVIEW

An online virtual reference workshop was developed at the College of Information Studies at the University of Maryland and delivered in Spring and Summer 2003 as part of an effort to identify effective online training techniques for virtual reference. Effective training was measured in several ways: overall satisfaction with the course, satisfaction with specific training techniques, preferences for specific training techniques, successful completion of hands-on exercises, and an increased confidence level in offering virtual reference services. The course design incorporated a variety of training techniques, including "cheat sheets," online tutorials, and telephone training. Based on an examination of a pre- and post-assessment and results of hands-on activities, the authors recommend an approach to incorporating hands-on practice for virtual reference, discuss prerequisite skills for training, identify challenges to offering this type of training and suggest future research for further development of effective training.

INTRODUCTION

Libraries of all types are offering real-time synchronous reference services in addition to in-person, e-mail, and telephone reference services. This type of reference service is referred to in the literature and in practice as virtual, or chat, reference. Virtual reference has extended the boundaries of reference services; state, regional, national and multinational consortia provide service 24 hours a day, seven days a week. Virtual reference service involves the application of reference skills in an electronic environment, simultaneously managing technology, searching for answers and communicating with patrons. Training programs for virtual reference focus on the use of software as well as the adaptation of reference skills to the new virtual environment; hands-on exercises are an important component. This chapter reports on efforts at the College of Information Studies at the University of Maryland to develop effective hands-on online training for virtual reference. The terms virtual and chat will be used interchangeably.

The importance of staff training for virtual reference services has been noted in the literature (Lipow, 2003; Salem, Balraj, and Lilly, 2003; Tucker, 2003). Developing successful training programs within one organization is challenging enough; the fact that chat reference service providers are not in a single location has complicated efforts to offer training. When addressing the training need within statewide, regional, national, or international consortia, issues become even more complex. Bromberg (2003) notes that a trainer for Q and A NJ, which has 33 libraries across the state of New Jersey, travels around the state to conduct training classes at various labs. Given the dispersed location of the reference service providers, online training programs could reach larger audiences and provide an opportunity for chat reference librarians around the world who collaborate to attend training sessions together.

Software vendors, reference staff members or coordinators, or a combination of all three have provided chat reference training. However, the amount and quality of vendor training varies among libraries and consortia (Coffman, 2003). One common approach has been to enlist the vendor to "train the trainer."

Approaches to training include hands-on training workshops, one-on-one mentoring, and on-the-job training. Delivery of the virtual reference training has been restricted primarily to in-person training, although Coffman (2003) noted the use of software meeting rooms and Web access plus speaker phones to train small groups of four to six people. Washington State combines an in-person workshop followed by hands-on activities (Hirko, 2003). Some vendors have prepared tutorials on CD-ROM and workbooks. Despite the different training models used, all of the virtual reference approaches provide hands-on practice, and the importance of this has been emphasized in the literature (Tunender and Horn, 2002; Harris, 2003).

A research team at the College of Information Studies at the University of Maryland, College Park, began to explore the delivery of online virtual reference training. Initially, a comprehensive online virtual reference training package was envisioned that would include a variety of topics: virtual reference software selection, beginning and intermediate reference skills, appropriateness of virtual reference in different organizations and settings, planning and implementing a virtual reference service, and legal issues in virtual reference. While focusing on virtual reference, several components covered basic reference skills and the online training techniques would be transferable to other types of reference services.

The first workshop was an introductory online virtual reference workshop titled Virtual Reference 1.0. This hands-on, highly interactive virtual reference workshop was developed in collaboration with LSSI[1] staff. The research team and LSSI staff delivered on the University of Maryland College Park campus in person twice in 2002. The workshop was then modified for the online environment by fleshing out PowerPoint presentations, transcribing lecture tapes, creating Web pages from handouts and developing customized orientation material. The course coordinator received support and access to instructional models from the Office of Instructional Technology, as well as graphic-design assistance. The biggest challenge is achieving precision for the complex instructions necessary to deliver this type of workshop. Nonlibrarians, as well as library and information science (LIS) graduate students reviewed the course material for clarity. The online workshop was delivered three times in 2003–2004; only the results of the first two offerings are reported here. The research was approved by the University of Maryland Institutional Review Board and workshop participants completed a research consent form.

The primary research question of this study focused on the feasibility of teaching librarians to use a sophisticated software package without face-to-face instruction. A secondary research question focused on the identification of effective online training techniques for virtual reference. For this study, effective training was measured in five ways:

- Overall satisfaction with the course, a traditional measure for all courses, and self-reporting measures
- Perceived effectiveness of specific training techniques
- Recommendations for specific training techniques, , and
- Confidence level in offering virtual reference services
- Successful completion of hands-on exercises, judged by the instructors based on successful login and utilization of software features

Evaluation of the performance itself was not considered.

A third research question related to the identification of characteristics of workshop participants that might predict success in the online virtual reference training environment. Before beginning the workshop, participants were asked to respond to a pre-assessment survey that elicited information about their technology and reference skills and experience, perceptions about virtual reference, and motivation for taking the course. In a post-assessment, participants evaluated the course as a whole, indicated satisfaction and preferences for specific training techniques, and provided perceptions about virtual reference.

DESCRIPTION OF WORKSHOP

This online workshop emphasized hands-on experience. Participants first learned how to use the technology with the goal of reaching a comfort level. Then, they reviewed or learned reference interview techniques and question-answering skills. Finally, workshop participants were asked to "pull it together" in a culminating exercise that combined use of the technology with execution of the reference skills. This approach is in line with the four areas of necessary skills described by Meola and Stormont (2002): core reference skills, real-time chat techniques, software-specific skills, and live virtual reference policies. In this workshop, participants have to learn software-specific skills, that is, which keyboard operations result in the desired outcomes, before they can focus on real-time chat techniques.

The four-week online workshop, offered using WebCT course management software was primarily asynchronous. Kraemer (2003) describes the features, benefits, and disadvantages of using course management software for training. Participants signed into the course space at specific times for individually scheduled exercises with classmate partners. Optional office hours, three hours weekly, were established for the first workshop but because of very low attendance, office hours were offered by appointment only after that. None were requested.

The techniques utilized in the hands-on workshop built on those used for in-person virtual reference training, such as role-playing (Sheets, 1998), "cheat sheets" (Salem, Balraj, and Lilly, 2003), and transcript analysis (Ward, 2003). In addition, other techniques were adapted for virtual reference training, including online tutorials developed with Viewlet Software and telephone-Web training sessions. Although various virtual reference software packages were discussed during the workshop, in order to facilitate training efforts, only one virtual reference software, Virtual Reference Toolkit (VRT), was used for the required hands-on exercises. Each participant was provided with his or her own unique logon id and individual queues for the duration of the workshop. They were encouraged to make unlimited use of the software and involve colleagues in supplementary practice sessions.

The workshop consisted of four modules; each module included specially prepared text, outside readings, and exercises. The workshop designers estimated that participants would spend ten hours on the workshop over the four-week period and receive one continuing education credit upon completion. These expectations were communicated to the participants in

the marketing materials and then again in the course orientation on WebCT. Table 3-1 gives an overview of the modules and
their objectives.

The first module, "The Virtual Reference Environment," introduced students to each other, to the WebCT environment, and
to basic concepts of virtual reference and professional resources.
In addition, participants signed into an existing virtual reference
service as a patron and reported their experience to others.

The second module, "Technology and Software," provided
an overview of the major types of chat technology and their

Table 3-1
Overview of Course Modules, Objectives, and Activities

Module	Objectives	Activities
Course Orientation	Familiarize participants with expectations for the course, the WebCT environment, and technical requirements	Complete research consent form and pre-assessment
1. The Virtual Reference Environment	Familiarity with WebCT, virtual reference principles, practice, and professional resources	Introductions, case study discussion, session initiation exercise and discussion
2. Technology and Software	Understanding of software options and features; introductory use of simple and VRT software	Software priorities survey, software discussion, use of simple chat software, training for VRT software, and login exercise
3. Quality Control	Identification of "best practices" and beneficial use of transcripts	Transcript analysis exercise
4. Role-Playing	Application of skills in simulation, self-assessment	Reference question exercise, role-playing discussion

respective features as well as hands-on training and practice. Participants reviewed software features and reflected on the importance of these features for specific user groups. The participants first practiced a reference interaction with a classmate using simple chat software, either AOL Instant Messenger or a chat feature available in WebCT. Participants then completed logon exercises using VRT software, both as a librarian and a patron. During the first workshop, partners were not assigned. Participants were asked to post a message about available times. That approach was overly burdensome, and in the later workshop, tentative partners were assigned. If the two people could not find a time to work together, the coordinator assisted in pairing people. In one of the workshops, a librarian in Baltimore worked in the afternoons with an Australian partner, very early on his "next morning."

In the third module, "Quality Control," participants learned to analyze transcripts to help improve reference services. Participants reviewed reference interview techniques, read award-winning transcripts, and critiqued real-life transcripts. The fourth and final module, "Role Playing," presented an opportunity for each participant to apply what he or she had learned in the earlier modules. In the first workshop, two exercises were included in the Role Playing module: an online catalog question and a reference scenario.

The first exercise required librarians to instruct the patron how to use any publicly available online catalog. Of interest, there were technical difficulties sending pages from some online catalogs, which were not anticipated by the instructors. In the evaluations of the first workshop, an overall response from participants was that the hours required by the course were higher than anticipated; for that reason, the "catalog question" was dropped from the second workshop.

The second exercise provided participants with a "reference scenario." Two scenarios were developed—one for each patron to use in asking a question. The scenario started with a "Type in this question" instruction. The rest of the scenario information was to be shared with the librarian only if he or she asked for the information during the reference interview. Information included in the scenario specified the reason for the request, the type of information needed, the background of the requester, and so on. This exercise provided each participant with an opportunity to practice a "real" reference interview in the virtual reference environment from both the perspective of a patron and of a librarian. Both scenarios were developed so that a reference interview was essential to understanding the patron's true information need; in other words, if the librarian took the request at face value, the true information would not be met. Partners could share the scenarios after the completion of the exercise so that the participant who was the librarian would know if he or she had arrived at the true information need. Afterwards, workshop participants posted reflections on their respective performances as they practiced managing the software, the interview, and the patron, all with a heightened sense of urgency.

While designing the workshop series, the authors identified several issues and concerns. First, it is not common for a school of library and information science (LIS) to offer this type of hands-on training. As noted above, virtual reference training is generally offered through vendors or staff or a combination of both. The role of LIS programs in virtual reference training was examined as the process unfolded.

Second, a university's being affiliated with one vendor for this training effort was examined closely. While VRT software was used, the focus of the workshop was on reference skills and not on the software. A distinction was drawn between marketing software and using software to complete hands-on exercises. The use of a particular vendor for teaching purposes is not unusual in library and information science programs. For example, Carol Tenopir (2001) discusses the use of Dialog as part of the master's degree in library sciences. In addition, several potential participants either used or were planning to use different virtual reference software in their libraries.

Third, technical difficulties were found to be very time consuming and presented obstacles in extending the hands-on training component. These problems occurred in both home and work environments. In addition, authentication and licensing issues arose as the hands-on exercises were developed. Reactions and recommendations related to these issues will be presented in the discussion section.

DESCRIPTION OF HANDS-ON TRAINING
OPPORTUNITIES

When the idea for this online course was conceived, there was some question about whether or not participants could learn to use a sophisticated software package without in-person training and its capacity to provide immediate feedback to both student and instructor. Multiple training approaches were made available to participants to accommodate various learning styles: "cheat sheets," online tutorials, telephone training. Individual phone support was available on request.

Cheat Sheets

"Cheat sheets" from both the patron and librarian perspectives were provided in two separate documents. This allowed participants to easily involve colleagues in practice sessions. Offered in downloadable PDF format, they included step-by-step instructions, color screen shots, scripted questions, and directed activities, such as "pushing a Web page" and sending a Power Point presentation.

Online Tutorials

Training material for VRT software was presented in the form of two online tutorials, both created with Viewlet software, a Qarbon product. A 13-minute version, created by the vendor, did not include sound; the other, 20 minutes in length, created by University of Maryland personnel, was customized for the course and offered voice instruction. It could be stopped and started at any point for as many showings as desired. This type of online tutorial has potential beyond virtual reference and can target library patrons as well as librarians. Daghita, Dudey, and Heekin (2002) discuss the use of Viewlet software to create Web-based training for customers.

Telephone Training

During the first workshop, an additional training option was offered in the form of telephone conference-call sessions led by vendor personnel. Three sessions were scheduled; one was cancelled because of low demand. In all, only 5 out of the 24 enrollees participated in the remaining two sessions. The option was discontinued in future offerings of the workshop because of the additional cost and minimal interest. The lack of interest in this "real time" training seemed to reinforce the importance of offering distance education anytime, anywhere through asynchronous methods.

Description of Discussion and Interaction with Colleagues

Each module provided opportunities for discussion with colleagues. Discussions are an important way to form a sense of community; however, too many discussions overwhelm the participants. Table 3-2 summarizes the opportunities for discussion during the workshop.

Table 3-2
Opportunities for Interaction with Other Workshop Participants

Module	Discussion topic
1. The Virtual Reference Environment	Introductions: Descriptions of professional background and interest in virtual reference Case-study discussion: Reactions to case studies read as part of the workshop requirements Session initiation: Discussion of reactions to being a patron on a virtual reference service
2. Technology and Software	Software discussion: Identification of priorities for software features
3. Quality Control	Transcript-analysis discussion: Identification of best and worst practices [Note: Changed to a survey format since short time frame made group discussion difficult]
4. Role-Playing	Role-playing discussion: Presentation of self-assessment, description of challenges and successes.

Description of Opportunities for Feedback from Instructors

Instructors and participants shared an e-mail system within WebCT for posing and answering individual questions. Outside e-mail addresses of instructors were provided in the event that participants could not sign into WebCT. Instructors promised and delivered 24-hour response time to both e-mail and discussion threads. A special discussion topic titled "Help!" was created for participants to post "emergency," usually technological, questions. In addition, the course coordinator provided phone support to participants who experienced technological problems; six participants used the telephone for trouble-shooting software glitches.

STUDY SAMPLE

The primary sample frame consisted of 47 participants who registered for the workshop during two different offerings. The workshop participants represented 17 different American states in four different time zones. There were two international enrollments. Only 25 of the 47 participants completed the pre- and post-assessments; the results presented in this chapter represent the 25 participants who completed both the exercises and the pre- and post-assessments. In addition, a three-credit e-reference course that was offered at the College of Information Studies during Summer 2003 and Summer 2004 included the same pre and post assessment surveys as well as the same training techniques. Results relating to preferences for training methods will include responses from 48 students who completed the pre- and post-assessments out of the 56 students enrolled in the course. Table 3-3 summarizes enrollment and exercise completion for both workshop participants and students.

The course design did not withhold content for failure to complete the pre-assessment and continuing education certificates were not withheld for failure to complete the post-assessment. Several requests were made to the workshop participants to complete both the pre- and post-assessments using WebCT discussion announcements and WebCT e-mail. A limitation of this study is the small sample size; for that reason, only descriptive

Table 3-3
Enrollment and Completion of Exercises and Assessments

	Enrolled	Completed exercises		Completed pre- and post-assessments	
	Number	Number	%	Number	%
Workshop April 2003	24	20	83%	10	42%
Workshop August 2003	23	21	91%	15	65%
Course Summer 2003	27	25	93%	25	93%
Course Summer 2004	28	26	93%	23	82%

statistics will be reported. Statistical tests were run to identify significant differences between workshop participants and students in the three-credit course.

PROFILE OF SUCCESSFUL PARTICIPANTS

The following analysis is based on those respondents who completed both the pre- and post-assessments. The respondents were employed in a cross-section of library types: 7 from academic; 5 from public; 5 from special; 4 from government agencies; 2 were not working; 2 indicated other. All but one participant had had reference experience. A vast majority (24 out of 25, 96%) indicated that they had at least a moderate level of experience at the reference desk; 18 out of 25 (72%) indicated that their level was either high or expert. Telephone reference expertise was somewhat lower, with 2 out of the 25 respondents indicating a low level of experience, and 22 out of 25 indicating at least a level of moderate or above. Experience with e-mail was high, with 22 out of 25 (88%) indicating at least a moderate level. Only two participants had offered virtual reference on a regular basis. Most participants (20 out of 25, 80%) had never taken a distance education course prior to the workshop. Most

(20 out of 25, 80%) had little or no experience with course-management software.

The participants self-assessed themselves as having at least an intermediate level of general computer technology usage (23 out of 25, 92%). They used e-mail regularly (22 out of 25, 88%), considered themselves highly experienced (or expert) in searching the Web (22 out of 25, 88%) and had moderate experience with listservs (15 out of 25 or 60%). Most respondents (18 out of 25, 72%) had at least moderate experience searching paid databases. However, most (17 out of 25, 68%) had little or no experience with chat technology. Even so, more than half of the respondents (16 out of 25, 64%) had at least a moderate level of confidence in their ability to conduct a virtual reference interview prior to taking the workshop. Before taking the workshop, more than half of the participants (17 out of 25, 68%) selected the word "stimulating" to describe how they felt about working in a multitasking environment.

The majority of participants (20 out of 25, 80%) decided on their own to take the workshop and in almost three-quarters of the registrations (18 out of 25, 72%), employers paid for the workshop. Nearly all (24 out of 25, 96%) expressed a high level of enthusiasm about the workshop before beginning. Although the group as a whole had little experience with distance education, it did not seem to be a barrier to effective participation. The participants were generally comfortable with other Web-based technologies, self-selected in terms of their interest in the workshop topic, and able to enroll without personal financial cost.

Since the results of the pre- and post-assessments for students enrolled in the three-credit e-reference course are included in some of the discussion, the students were compared to the workshop participants in terms of computer and reference experience and abilities. As would be expected, the workshop participants had significantly more experience in the provision of reference service at the reference desk and by telephone. However, there was not significant difference in experience with virtual reference. There was no significant difference in the confidence level of conducting a virtual reference interview in the pre-assessment. Students and workshop participants were also similar in their overall ability to use computer technology; there were no significant differences in their use of e-mail and chat or in their ability to search the Web. Students had more experience with course-management software and listservs.

FINDINGS

The effectiveness of the workshop was measured in several ways. The post-assessment provided the participants with the opportunity to evaluate various aspects of the workshop, to express their satisfaction with the workshop, and to assess their abilities. In addition, completion of hands-on exercises was considered to be an important measure of success. Of the total number of workshop participants, 41 out of 47 (87%) completed the hands-on exercises. The six who did not complete the exercises were not engaged in overall workshop activities for various reasons, i.e., did not review much content or post to many of the discussions. At least four of the six participants were overwhelmed by work responsibilities that peaked at the time of the workshop offering. One person was traveling internationally and did not have the Internet access she had expected. The sixth person, who had chat reference experience, was more interested in the training techniques than in the course content itself. All of the workshop participants who completed both the pre- and post-assessments completed the hands-on exercises. The completion rates for the two workshops, which can be seen in Table 3-3, were 83% and 93%. Given the high drop-out rate in distance-education courses noted by Hirko (2004: 24), these completion rates are high and seem to be a positive indicator of overall course design.

Fifty-one out of the 56 students enrolled in the three-credit e-reference course completed the hands-on exercises. Of the five who did not complete the exercises, four did not complete the course requirements by the end of the course, either dropping the course or taking an incomplete for the course. One student did not complete the exercises, and to the knowledge of the instructors, did not attempt to access VRT during the course.

In addition to exercise completion, participant perceptions were important measures of the success of the workshop. Participants were asked to rate the quality of the appropriateness of the course content for their needs. More than half of the respondents (13 out of 25, 52%) rated the course content as excellent; another 9 participants (36%) indicated that the content was very good; 3 participants rated the course content as good. No respondents rated the content below good. Twenty-two of the participants (88%) indicated that they would recommend this workshop to a colleague and 3 indicated that they might; no participants said that they would not recommend the workshop.

Participants were asked to indicate their satisfaction with various aspects of the workshop: discussion opportunities, feedback from instructors, interaction with classmates, and hands-on opportunities. Table 3-4 presents the various satisfaction ratings. The majority of respondents were either satisfied or very satisfied with all of the aspects of the workshop. One participant was very dissatisfied with both personal effort and discussion opportunities. This participant noted in a comment: "I have no suggestions on improvement on your end. Improvement would best be addressed on my end in terms of having all the components in place before attempting the exercises. The firewall issues need to be addressed before attempting to complete the course." This comment highlights the impact of technological issues and demonstrates the importance of preplanning and flexibility in trouble-shooting problems that arise. The participant who was somewhat dissatisfied with the amount of personal attention noted:

> The frustration I experienced with the pace of the course is inherent in (my reaction to) distance learning as an instructional vehicle, and is not specific to this class. The inability to get timely feedback made the learning curve seem unnecessarily long—questions that could have been answered instantly in a classroom setting took days to clarify, with concomitant loss of efficiency when you are trying to troubleshoot software, solve problems, and maximize a learning experience. I believe this course probably made an excellent [in person] workshop, but is less satisfying in this mode. The telephone conference call w/ a trainer in Module 1 was a highlight; the limited office hours were a problem; and the message traffic from course monitors was a valiant (but I think ultimately insufficient) effort to make up for shortfalls in "hands-on" personalized training.

Table 3-4
Participant Satisfaction with Various Aspects of the Workshop

	Personal satisfaction		Discussion opportunities		Personal attention		Interaction with classmates		Feedback		Hands-on	
	No.	%	No.	%	No.	%	No.	%	No.	%	No.	%
Very dissatisfied	1	4%	1	4%	0	–	0	–	0	–	0	–
Somewhat dissatisfied	0	–	0	–	1	4%	2	8%	0	–	2	8%
Neutral	0	–	2	8%	2	8%	5	20%	5	20%		–
Satisfied	15	60%	13	52%	4	16%	16	64%	7	28%	4	16%
Very satisfied	9	36%	9	36%	18	72%	2	8%	13	52%	19	76%
Total	25		25		25		25		25		25	

Of the various components of the course, satisfaction with the hands-on component was the highest, with 19 out 25 (76%) respondents indicating that they were very satisfied with the hands-on component. The two participants who indicated that they were somewhat satisfied with the hands-on practice both experienced technological problems. One noted: "Being an overseas student, I found the technology in the past few weeks due to all the worm virus attacks was very slow at times and er[r]atic." And the other recommended: "It would be a good idea as part of the application for the course to include questions about your Internet access and firewalls." Several participants indicated that the hands-on practice was the most valuable component of the workshop. One participant noted: "I think I learned just as much by being the patron and seeing some of the cues that were overlooked by the librarian." This statement supported Ronan's (2003) comment that role-playing as a patron strengthens reference skills.

Participants were asked to rate the effectiveness of the two primary means used to provide instruction for use of virtual reference software. As can be seen in Table 3-5, all workshop participants who used the cheat sheets and online tutorials found them to be somewhat effective or very effective. Of the 14 respondents who found the cheat sheets and online tutorials to be very effective, 8 of the respondents found both the cheat sheets and online tutorial to be very effective, 6 found the cheat sheets very effective, and 6 the online tutorials. Also shown in Table 3-5 are the responses from the students enrolled in the three-credit course. Three students did not find the cheat sheets effective, and one student did not find the online tutorial effective. However, there is no significant difference in satisfaction between students in the course and workshop participants.

In addition, workshop participants were asked to recommend a method or combination of methods for providing instructions for use of virtual reference software. Only two of these methods were used in the class, the other methods listed are those known to have been used for virtual reference training. Since the students did not directly experience these training methods in this workshop, the question is hypothetical, aiming to obtain the participants' perceptions.

- Eighteen out of 25 participants recommended using cheat sheets in combination with other methods; no participants recommended the use of "cheat sheets" as a sole means of training.

Table 3-5
Satisfaction with Cheat Sheets and Online Tutorials
(Number of Respondents)

	Cheat sheets				Online tutorials			
	Workshop		Course		Workshop		Course	
Did not use	0	–	2	4%	1	4%	2	4%
Totally useless	0	–	0	–	0	–	0	–
Not very effective	0	–	3	6%	0	–	1	2%
Somewhat effective	11	44%	24	50%	10	40%	20	42%
Very effective	14	56%	19	40%	14	56%	25	52%
Total	25		48		25		48	

- Sixteen participants recommended using Web and voice in combination with other methods; 2 participants recommended training with Web and voice alone.
- Sixteen recommended use of online tutorials in combination with other means; 1 participant recommended using online tutorials as a sole means of training.
- Three recommended face-to-face training as the sole means of training.

More than one participant recommended the following specific combinations of training methods:

- cheat sheets, online tutorials, Web and voice training, and face-to-face training (7 respondents)
- cheat sheets and online tutorials (3 respondents)
- online tutorials, Web and voice training, and video (3 respondents)

Another measure of workshop effectiveness was the participant's level of confidence to conduct a virtual reference interview after completing the workshop. Workshop participants were asked about their confidence level both before the workshop in the pre-assessment and after completing the workshop in the post-assessment. As can be seen in Table 3-6, after completing the workshop, no participants felt that their ability was very

Table 3-6
Confidence in Ability to Conduct a Virtual Reference Interview

	Pre-Assessment		Post-Assessment	
	Number	%	Number	%
Very high	0	–	4	16%
High	4	16%	16	64%
Moderate	12	48%	4	16%
Low	6	24%	1	4%
Very low	3	12%	0	–
Total	25		25	

low; approximately 80% of the respondents (20 out of 25) rated their ability as high or very high after the workshop as compared to 16% (4 out of 25) prior to the workshop. Prior to the workshop, no respondents rated their ability to conduct a virtual reference interview as very high; after completing the workshop, 4 participants (16%) rated their ability as very high.

The workshop exposed participants to multitasking, a capacity that has been called essential to virtual reference, not only because of the nature of virtual reference but also because it helps librarians understand the behavior of college students and younger information seekers, who often run more than one program or Web browser simultaneously (Ronan, 2003). It was expected that participants might learn more about their preference for virtual reference based at least in part on their reaction to multitasking. There was a slight increase in the number of respondents who described multitasking as enjoyable and stimulating following the workshop; on the other hand, there are also a few more respondents who described multitasking as stressful after completing the workshop.

There was no notable change in either preferred means of providing reference service or in the least preferred means although there was some indication that respondents felt more favorable toward chat reference after the workshop. Prior to the workshop, only 1 respondent preferred virtual reference and after the workshop, 3 respondents preferred virtual reference. Prior to the workshop, 2 respondents indicated that virtual reference was their least favorite means of providing reference service. After the workshop, no respondents selected virtual reference as least favorite; 6 additional respondents indicated that they had no least favorite means following the workshop.

An analysis of attitude toward multitasking and preference for reference service did not yield any notable patterns. As was noted above, no participants selected virtual reference as their least favorite type of reference service, even the participants who found multitasking to be stressful. Along similar lines, of the 20 participants who found multitasking enjoyable or stimulating, only 2 selected virtual reference as their preferred form of reference.

DISCUSSION AND RECOMMENDATIONS

The following discussion will first address the three primary research questions and then discuss various training issues that need to be resolved for online virtual reference training to be viable.

Is online virtual reference training feasible?

Based on the results of this study, the researchers concluded that it is feasible to offer online virtual reference training. All workshop participants and students who made an effort to complete the workshop or the course were successful in utilizing sophisticated virtual reference software as part of the hands-on exercises.

What are effective techniques for online virtual reference training?

To be successful, the online course should provide a variety of different training techniques to meet different learning styles. No one method emerged as a sole preferred means of virtual reference training. Both cheat sheets and online tutorials, the two training techniques used in the workshop are recommended for online virtual reference training. This research project did not gather specific comments about the two training tools; future assessments will ask for suggestions for improvement to see if the cheat sheet and online tutorial can be improved to increase satisfaction. Responses indicate that workshop participants are interested in Web and voice training sessions; however, in testing this method in the first workshop, the actual attendance at those sessions was low. Since the two asynchronous methods were successful in teaching virtual reference skills, their flexibility seems to make them preferred alternatives for training.

It is important that a person be "on call" to respond to technical difficulties. E-mail seems to work well, as long as the turnaround time is quick. The ability to talk to an instructor, when necessary, is a good feature in cases in which problems or misunderstandings arise.

Because hands-on practice requires working with another person, the structure of the course should offer flexibility in completing the exercises. Assigning partners is preferable; if the partners are not able to find a convenient time to "meet," alternative partners can be identified. Allowing some of the exercises to be completed with individuals not enrolled in the workshop seems to reduce some of the issues involved in scheduling hands-on exercises.

How much is enough hands-on practice?

A related question to training methods is to determine the appropriate type and how much hands-on training to offer. As was noted in the workshop description, the initial workshop offering seemed to have too many hands-on requirements. The objective of the hands-on exercises needs to be kept in perspective. Students in this workshop are not expected to be experts in the use of the software but rather conversant with skill requirements. Role-playing as both librarian and patron is essential and should be factored into the design of exercises. The number of hours of hands-on exercises should be determined in relation to the length of the workshop overall. In our case, this was calculated in relation to Continuing Education Credits which require 1 hour of class time for each .1 Continuing Education Credit. In addition, it is not expected that the learning process ends with the workshop but rather the workshop should serve as the beginning of learning about virtual reference. Coffman (2003) reminds us that virtual reference training is never complete; the skills must be used to be maintained at a high level.

Is there a profile of students likely to succeed in online virtual reference training?

Online learning is not for every one. All of the workshop participants and students in this study who completed the pre- and post-assessment had at least an intermediate level of computer expertise. This seems to be an important requirement for students interested in online virtual reference training or education. The level of reference experience does not seem to be a factor for an introductory-level virtual reference course. While the workshop participants had some reference experience, in-person, telephone, or e-mail, most of the students in the e-reference class did not.

Two important considerations are attitude toward distance learning and time commitment. The pre-assessment did not capture participants' perceptions about online courses, only prior experience with online courses. A question about attitude toward online education will be added to the pre- and post-assessments to determine if, in fact, this is a factor that influences a student's success. It is clear that online education is not effective for everyone. However, even students who do not enjoy the online training environment can learn the needed skills.

In addition to a positive attitude toward online training, students of online courses need to understand that online courses demand the same level of attention and time commitment as face-to-face training. The expectations need to be clear and accurate. In this case, the orientation section of the workshop stated the time commitment required to complete all activities. However, this information should be clearly communicated to participants in marketing materials prior to registration. Because instructors seem to have the tendency to underestimate the time commitment, it would be helpful to have the workshop participants systematically track how much time they spend on the exercises. As was noted above, the participants in the first offering of the workshop made it very clear that the time commitment far exceeded the advertised time requirements. However, in addition to the need for computer competencies, emphasis should be given to self-motivation and time-management skills. Marketing materials might include a statement that successful completion of the course requires these qualities.

TRAINING ISSUES

This online training project raised several issues, including technological challenges and questions about the roles of the various stakeholders in providing training. The issues identified relate to training and may or may not apply to library and information science education.

Technological issues are not trivial. The virtual reference software continues to favor certain platforms and the configuration demands are high. There was a five-page set of instructions in a PDF file on how to configure a browser for software. Some options required participants to communicate with members of their respective information technology staff. In addition,

WebCT had its own set of instructions. Organizational firewalls present additional barriers to the success of online training. One possible solution is to send the configuration instructions as soon as participants register for the workshop so that they have more time to work out any problems they encounter so that once the workshop begins, they can focus on the course content. It is difficult, if not impossible, to foresee the various technological issues that will arise. Technical support is key to success, both from the workshop provider as well as from the participants' organizations. In addition, an intermediate level of computer experience will help ensure that technological issues will be resolved quickly.

Another issue related to virtual reference software is the selection of software for training. Obviously, vendors offer training for the software they sell. Libraries and information centers want to train their staff on the software that they will use. Offering access to multiple virtual reference desk software places a burden on the trainer to tailor training materials to each of the software packages used and to develop trouble-shooting expertise for each. Yet to attract a wider audience, this would be required. Several prospective workshop attendees requested access to virtual reference desk software that had been selected in their organizations.

In addition to virtual reference software issues, there are technological challenges related to offering advanced training that would require the use of licensed fee-based databases. While free online resources are used to respond to virtual reference questions, the use of fee-based resources may be preferred. Licensing restriction and authentication requirements limit the use of fee-based databases in training across institutional boundaries. It should be noted that this issue transcends online virtual reference training and applies to virtual reference service provision when the librarian and the patron are working in different networks.

The various issues identified above suggest roles for each of the stakeholders in virtual reference training: the vendors, the organizations, and universities. The best approach to online virtual reference training will be through partnerships. Organizations that have already selected virtual reference software would do well to organize training sessions with the vendor. Various levels of training can be offered, including update and refresher sessions. Universities have a role to play in supplementing vendor software-specific skill training, with the transfer of core reference skills to the online environment and in highlighting and synthesizing key issues, such as legal issues in virtual reference. University training would be useful for organizations that have not selected a virtual reference platform or that are more interested in reference skills than in software utilization. Universities can also reach librarians who are not currently working in reference or in a library offering chat service. Universities may not be able to provide high-level skill training to a diverse set of participants and cannot keep librarians up to date on organization-specific policies or software upgrades.

CONCLUSIONS

Virtual reference services continue to grow and the demand for training increases with that growth. The dispersed location of libraries participating in statewide, national and international consortia presents challenges to the development of training programs. Effective online virtual reference training could help reach a broader audience. Based on the results of a small study, online hands-on virtual reference training is viable. Successful participants need some computer experience, a flexible approach to technology issues and a positive attitude toward online training. Asynchronous training methods are recommended for online training since they increase flexibility for participants. Both cheat sheets and online tutorials are somewhat effective but there is room for improvement of these training tools. Successful training programs will build partnerships that involve libraries, vendors, and universities.

NOTE

1. Tutor.com acquired the LSSI Reference Division in June 2003. Included in the acquisition was the LSSI Virtual Reference Toolkit. The software is now referred to as the Virtual Reference Toolkit.

REFERENCES

Bromberg, Peter. 2003. "Managing a Statewide Virtual Reference Service: How Q and A NJ Works." *Computers in Libraries* 23, no. 4 (April) : 26+

Coffman, Steve. 2003. *Going Live: Starting and Running a Virtual Reference Service.* Chicago: American Library Association.

Daghita, Joan, Kathryn Dudey, and Janet Heekin. 2002. "E-Training: Meeting the Users on Their Terms." Putting Knowledge to Work. Papers Presented at the Special Libraries Association Conference (June 9-12), Los Angeles, CA.

Harris, Lydia. 2003. "Software is Not Enough: Teaching and Training Digital Reference Librarians." Presentation at the Virtual Reference Desk Conference 2003, Charting the Course for Reference. San Antonio, Texas.

Hirko, Buff, and Mary Bucher Ross. 2004. Virtual Reference Training: The Complete Guide to Providing Anytime, Anywhere Answers. Chicago: American Library Association.

Kraemer, Elizabeth W. 2003. "Developing the Online Learning Environment: The Pros and Cons of Using WebCT for Library Instruction." *Information Technology and Libraries* 22, no. 2: 87–92.

Lipow, Anne Grodzins. 2003. *Virtual Reference Librarian's Handbook.* Berkeley, CA: Library Solutions Press.

Meola, Mark, and Sam Stormont. 2002. *Starting and Operating Live Virtual Reference Services.* New York: Neal-Schuman.

Ronan, Jana Smith. 2003. *Chat Reference: A Guide to Live Virtual Reference Services.* Westport, CT: Libraries Unlimited.

Salem, Joseph, Leela Balraj, and Erica Lilly. 2003. "Real-Time Training for Virtual Reference." Presented at the Virtual Reference Desk Conference, The Reference Roundup (November), San Antonio, TX, www.vrd2003.org/proceedings/presentation.cfm?PID=214 (accessed October 18, 2005).

Sheets, Janet E. (1998). "Role-Playing as a Training Tool for Reference Student Assistants." *Reference Services Review* 26, no. 1: 37–41

Tenopir, Carol. 2001. "Why I still Teach Dialog." *Library Journal* 126, no. 8: 35 +

Tucker, James Cory. 2003. "Developing a Chat Reference Training Program." *Internet Reference Services Quarterly* 8, no. 4: 11–25

Tunender, Heather, and Judy Horn. 2002. "Bringing It All Together: Training for Integrating Electronic Reference." Presentation at the Virtual Reference Desk Conference, Charting the Course for Reference: Toward a Preferred Future (November), Chicago, www.vrd.org/conferences/VRD2002/proceedings/tunender-horn.shtml.

Ward, David. 2003. Using Virtual Reference Transcripts for Staff Training. *Reference Services Review* 31, no. 1: 45–56.

Chapter 4

Staffing for Live Electronic Reference: Balancing Service and Sacrifice

Joe Blonde

OVERVIEW

Decisions about staffing for virtual reference are often impro-
vised according to a library's organizational culture. To encourage broader perspectives, information about staffing practices
for chat reference was gathered from a survey of 16 Canadian
university libraries. Data is presented on categories of staff, staff
participation and deployment, service hours, and coordination
of chat reference for individual libraries and libraries in a consortium. The survey confirms that large numbers of staff have
been mobilized for chat reference without recourse to hiring or
reassignment. Developing a sustainable staffing model is a challenge especially for libraries with limited staffing flexibility.
Lack of recognition of workload implications may undermine
the efforts of those trying to meet that challenge.

INTRODUCTION

The promise of real-time, computer-based reference service available to people no matter where they are located is a compelling

vision for librarians. What was not long ago a science-fiction fantasy, the seamless interface that enables a full range of digital reference practices, now seems not that far away. Chat reference has already opened a new channel of communication to remote users that has been augmented by escorting and cobrowsing applications. Can there be any doubt that within the next generation live virtual reference will become as ubiquitous as e-mail reference? Nevertheless, the initial enthusiasm for chat reference as the herald of a new era of online library services has come under increasing scrutiny. The risks for libraries of putting too many eggs in the chat basket without achieving a reasonable volume of interactions have been raised with persuasive candor. (Coffman and Arret, 2004). The staffing commitment needed to launch and sustain a chat reference service can easily be underestimated. Academic librarians caught up in their eagerness to experiment with online reference may be overlooking some of the sacrifice of time and money that it entails. The challenge of developing a workable staffing model for chat reference ought to be front and center in the planning process.

It is logical to assume that decisions about staffing for virtual reference are rooted in the organizational culture of individual libraries. Every library has its own story to tell about how its chat reference service began and how it has evolved. While training and competency development receive much of the attention in the literature, the participation and deployment of staff are typically considered local issues. Although some research has surveyed staffing practices for virtual reference, most notably the ARL survey done in the summer of 2002, most of the information on the number and categories of staff involved comes from individual case studies and evaluation reports. The ARL survey gathered responses from over 60 academic libraries on staff categories, hours of service, coordination, and other staffing issues (Ronan and Turner, 2002) Its findings provided considerable evidence to support the conclusion that "chat reference is an extremely dynamic new area of library service." (Ronan and Turner, 2002:14) Recent books on chat reference have examined the question of devising appropriate staffing models, offering much valuable insight on the relative merits of different approaches. (Meola and Stormont, 2002; Ronan, 2003)

As service schedules are often based on longstanding practice within an institution, staffing chat reference as an additional service point poses a serious challenge. Unless participation is entirely voluntary, existing staff must be persuaded to revise their workload. To achieve a staffing model that can be sustained over the long term, academic libraries embarking on live electronic reference must deal with the complicated task of redistributing workload to accommodate virtual reference while maintaining existing in-person services. How Canadian academic libraries are handling this task was the subject of a survey carried out in September and October 2004. The coordinators of virtual reference services in Canadian university libraries were contacted and interviewed by telephone, using a questionnaire to elicit information on staffing practices. Questions about hours of chat coverage, categories, and numbers of staff were supplemented by questions that probed into the background and organization of the service. Each interview provided a snapshot of chat reference practice in the individual library and yielded some data that could be used for comparative purposes.

At the time this survey was conducted, 18 of the 27 academic libraries belonging to the Canadian Association of Research Libraries (CARL) were providing virtual reference services using chat. Data from 16 respondents were compiled for this study, all from CARL institutions except for one. Though not a member of CARL, the single exception was affiliated with other CARL libraries in a small consortium. Findings confirmed how quickly staff resources have been mobilized to offer chat reference in these academic libraries. Such rapid growth in a new service area suggests that many academic librarians in Canada have acknowledged the importance of building virtual reference infrastructures and are actively engaged in the development of Internet-based reference services.

TYPES OF SERVICE

Based on the premise that staffing practices in libraries that belong to virtual reference consortia could be different from those in libraries only serving their own university communities,

Table 4-1
Type of Service

Type of service	Number of libraries
Individual library	10
Small consortium	5
Large consortium	1

three types of service were identified: individual libraries, small consortia of two to four libraries, and large consortia of five or more libraries. Table 4-1 shows the distribution by type with the largest number being individual libraries. Going it alone was the choice of the majority, at least in part, because organizational issues are more easily resolved at a local level. Several respondents mentioned the willingness of their library administrators to back in-house projects.

The ability to offer more hours of chat reference coverage was the most often cited rationale for the six libraries involved in consortia. Four of the six had initially engaged in chat service as individual libraries before joining a consortium. The development of consortia in Canada is not as widespread as in the United States, where state library associations play a key role in providing funding and organizational support to cooperative initiatives. Only recently have provincially based cooperative endeavors for chat reference started up in several Canadian provinces.

Chat reference was considered a regular service in 12 of the libraries surveyed, whereas 4 viewed it as a pilot or special project. This rapid passage to regularization indicates a surprising level of acceptance for chat despite its labor-intensive nature. Even though the inception of chat services dates back no further than two or three years, this new medium of virtual interaction has quickly established its place in academic reference. Since the cost of purchasing chat reference technology is now relatively low, there are no obvious barriers to implementation as long as existing staff are prepared to take it on. Indeed, the survey found that special funding has not been instrumental in the establishment of chat reference. Only one of the libraries reported receiving significant funds from outside the regular library budget.

SERVICE HOURS

Data were collected on the hours of chat coverage in each library with a view towards uncovering any patterns relating to staffing levels. Coverage was grouped into weekday and weekend segments and charted separately for individual libraries and for libraries in consortia. The amount of coverage was also measured against a 58-hour weekday mean and a 12-hour weekend mean, representing a reasonable standard for walk-in reference coverage in academic libraries. The means functioned as a crude measure of comparison for chat reference with traditional in-person reference service. Tables 4-2 and 4-3 show the range of weekday coverage for individual libraries and for libraries in consortia respectively.

Surprisingly, the range of chat coverage hours for libraries in consortia did not differ greatly from that of individual libraries, except for the one library offering 24/7 coverage. Four

Table 4-2
Hours of Coverage for Individual Libraries

Individual library	Weekday hours	Percentage of mean (58 hours)	Weekend hours	Percentage of mean (12 hours)
A	65	112%	14	117%
B	56	97%	10	83%
C	51	88%	18	150%
D	51	88%	10	83%
E	40	69%	0	–
F	36	62%	0	–
G	30	52%	0	–
H	30	52%	0	–
I	20	34%	0	–
J	15	26%	0	–

Table 4-3
Hours of Coverage for Libraries in Consortia

Library	Weekday hours	Percentage of mean (58 hours)	Weekend hours	Percentage of mean (12 hours)
K	120	207%	48	400%
L	50	86%	0	–
M	50	86%	0	–
N	50	86%	0	–
O	32	55%	8	67%
P	32	55%	8	67%

of the ten individual libraries were able to provide over 50 hours of weekday coverage, exceeding the amount of coverage in most of the libraries in a consortium. Eight of the ten individual libraries attained at least 50% of the weekday mean, basically keeping pace with the performance of the libraries in a consortium. The capacity of individual libraries to offer extensive hours of coverage brings into question the assumption that cooperative arrangements are required to make longer chat service hours possible.

Most of the libraries surveyed, 14 of 16, were offering at least 30 hours of weekday chat coverage, and half of the libraries provided over 45 hours of coverage, exceeding 80% of the 58-hour weekday mean. Both individual libraries and libraries in consortia appreciated the necessity of providing extensive coverage in order to encourage greater usage. Covering the busiest hours, particularly in the evenings, was frequently mentioned as a basis for modifying service hours. Most of those interviewed had made adjustments to their coverage and reviewed usage statistics for this purpose. Six libraries closed their chat service during the summer, and others reduced hours during intersessions. With one exception, 24/7 coverage was not considered the best option to setting service hours.

Service on weekends was emphasized less. Nine of the sixteen libraries have no service at all on weekends. Even three of the six libraries in a consortium have no weekend service.

Five libraries provided ten or more hours of weekend coverage, exceeding 80% of the 12-hour mean. Only one of those five was a library in a consortium. Given standard academic practice, which excludes weekend classes and reduces academic service, several survey respondents alluded to the lack of available staff on weekends. The libraries providing weekend coverage were usually able to call on part-time staff, student librarians, and graduate assistants.

Generally the availability of staff was most often mentioned as the crucial factor in determining service hours. Although other considerations were taken into account, including Web traffic reports; the flexibility of staffing options was the pivotal factor for most respondents. To extend service hours, 12 respondents indicated they would need additional staff. Only 2 of the 16 thought that they could manage more coverage with their existing staff. As expected, libraries with the largest overall number of staff have more potential for expanding service hours, although coordination and training tend to become more complex.

STAFF CATEGORIES AND WORKLOAD

Table 4-4 shows the mix of staff categories engaged in chat reference in 15 of the 16 libraries surveyed. One library did not supply data. Nine libraries utilized at least two categories while six relied exclusively on librarians. Of the 9 libraries using a mix of categories, 8 utilized nonprofessional staff, and four engaged student librarians or graduate assistants. However librarians dominated the mix in all but 4 of the 16 libraries making up more than 70% of the total staffing compliment across all institutions. When asked to explain their practice, the response most often given was that it followed the same pattern as the regular reference desk staffing. The prevalence of librarians suggests that chat reference is seen as a professional service requiring staff with well-developed reference skills. Where nonprofessional staff were used, they were mostly senior library assistants who had extensive experience answering reference questions. Student librarians and graduate assistants were generally engaged to extend hours of coverage on weekends or in the evening.

Table 4-4
Staff Categories

Library	Librarians	Nonprofessionals	Students/Interns
A	6	4	
B	6	8	4
C	19		5
E	5	1	1
F	7	8	
G	14	4	
H	22		
I	17		
J	9		
K	14	22	4
L	20		
M	11	3	
N	5	5	
O	11		
P	15		
TOTAL	181	55	14

The numbers of staff utilized for chat reference varied greatly—from 7 to 40—according to the overall size of the libraries. The average for libraries in consortia was 18 and the average for individual libraries was 16. Most libraries drew staff exclusively from reference or public service divisions, although six libraries also used librarians from other sectors, either technical services or library systems. Computer workstations used for chat reference were located in the staff offices in 15 of the 16 libraries. Two libraries had dedicated workstations although neither of these was located at the reference desk. Four libraries had arrangements for staff to work on chat from their homes.

Hours of service were distributed equally among the permanent staff in a majority of libraries although a few had dedicated staff who covered more of the shifts, or part-timers who worked the evenings and weekends. The length of chat reference shifts varied from one to four hours with two-hour shifts the most prevalent. According to several respondents, regular shift rotation was considered vital to maintaining familiarity with the chat software and protocols. Schedules for chat reference were adapted to local practice. Six libraries employed a weekly schedule, two libraries used a daily schedule, and two had a monthly schedule. There were other approaches to scheduling as well, including rotation by service unit, permanent slots, and fill-in electronic schedules. In most cases scheduling of chat had been integrated into the overall reference schedule and was not handled separately.

Based on the survey findings, hiring new staff to take up virtual reference duties is an uncommon practice. On the whole, reference departments have implemented chat service using existing staff. While two of the libraries surveyed had hired new full-time staff to assume virtual reference responsibilities, the remaining 14 libraries had not enlarged their permanent staff. Twelve of sixteen coordinators claimed that current service hours could be handled with existing staff. Of course, greater flexibility in setting hours was available to those able to call upon part-time and student librarians for virtual reference work.

In most cases, the time spent engaged in chat reference represented an additional workload. The portrait that emerged from the survey suggested willing volunteers eager to participate in chat reference, broad distribution of hours among them, productivity gains occurring through multitasking, and integration of chat as a response to the changing context of reference service. The devotion of academic librarians and library staff to reference service is likely concealing the magnitude of this increased workload. When asked whether chat reference shifts were considered equivalent to shifts worked at the reference desk, most of those interviewed responded that chat shifts were taken into consideration but not necessarily on an equivalent basis. Chat reference was recognized in workload assignments in only four of the 16 libraries, and just one library has incorporated the task into job descriptions. This indicates a disturbing lag in recognition for the legitimacy of virtual reference work. Will library administrators be willing to consider virtual reference as a major component in the hiring or reassignment

of library staff as long as this work goes largely unacknowl-
edged? How can this work be measured to give a better indication of staffing needs?

PARTICIPATION AND COORDINATION

The question of whether everyone who provides in-person reference service in an academic library should be obligated to staff
virtual reference services is subject to some debate. When everyone is encouraged to participate and the number of willing volunteers matches or exceeds the number of staff required, there
should be no major obstacle to developing a good staffing plan.
In other cases it is more difficult to assess the extent to which peer
pressure and organizational culture coerce people into participating. Of course, this can also be a matter of library policy insofar
as chat reference is viewed as a venue of service sanctioned by
administrative control. The recently issued Reference and User
Services Association (RUSA) *Guidelines* suggest that "library staff
conducting virtual reference should be selected on the basis of
ability, interest, and availability." (RUSA, 2004: 12) In this survey
11 libraries claimed they allowed voluntary participation as op-
posed to 5 libraries in which participation was assigned. When
asked to comment on the attitudes of staff, a sizeable majority of
those interviewed felt their staff members were enthusiastic
about chat reference irrespective of whether they had volunteered or not. They tended to link any dissatisfaction to factors
other than the freedom to choose whether or not to participate.

The attitudes and reactions of library staff to chat reference
are influenced by many factors, including training, comfort
level, frequency of shifts, software reliability and ease of use,
volume of business, work style, and the outcome of chat interactions. Though most of those interviewed indicated that staffs
were generally supportive and enthusiastic, nearly half con-
ceded that opinion was divided among their staff as to the value
of chat reference service. One respondent indicated that several
staff members had become disenchanted and opted out of chat
service. At my own library, an internal staff survey conducted
after the first year of operation showed a significant difference
of opinion among librarians as to the value of chat reference.

The task of coordinating virtual reference services is usually taken on by a reference librarian. According to survey responses, in 13 of the 16 libraries the coordinator was a librarian with other responsibilities. Eleven of these thirteen librarians were reference librarians. For the remaining three libraries, one coordinator was a librarian manager, one was a nonprofessional, and one was a librarian specializing in digital learning. This specialist librarian was the sole example of a position that explicitly recognized virtual reference coordination. Otherwise, the task of coordination constituted additional responsibilities for someone with another job description. When asked to estimate the percentage of time spent on coordinating, most responded that it was 25% or less, with highs and lows throughout the year.

While a strong argument for creating new digital reference coordinator positions is not supported by these findings, there is evidence to suggest that at least some of the responsibilities of coordination are often shared amongst a group of people. Some coordinators could delegate certain responsibilities or share them with colleagues. Scheduling and Web-site configuration were examples of tasks not frequently handled by the majority of coordinators. For libraries in consortia, coordinators could not only share responsibility for certain tasks but also had opportunities to discuss the overall planning and development of chat reference services with their counterparts in other institutions. For individual libraries, there were some examples of rotating the coordinator role among a group of librarians.

CONCLUSION

Building a sustainable staffing component for live online reference service is a critical challenge according to those interviewed for this survey. Most appeared to believe that, with proper training and support, their libraries would continue to rely on existing staff to deliver such services. None seemed to be considering outsourcing as an option for staffing. In answer to the final survey question, "Do you feel that chat reference is a sustainable service for the next five years?" 9 of the 16 coordinators replied in the affirmative. Some observed that an irreversible shift to the use of electronic information resources has already propelled chat towards becoming a basic reference service. The seven who responded that they were not convinced that chat reference would endure in its present form attributed their uncertainty to the low volume of traffic in their libraries as well as problems with existing chat reference technologies. However, even these skeptics were optimistic that "something" will be there five years from now.

In order to progress beyond a precarious balancing of virtual and traditional reference coverage with available staff, workload recognition of virtual reference duties would, in my view, help to establish chat reference on a firmer footing. Devising a method with which to calculate the appropriate number and category of staff needed to provide significant chat reference coverage would also benefit libraries planning to maintain and develop their virtual reference capabilities.

Usage data, especially times of peak demand, certainly needs to be factored in. Though an attempt was made to collect usage data in this survey, it was too fragmentary to support any useful analysis in regard to staffing.

Though barely three or four years old at most, chat reference service in these 16 libraries has already achieved significant outcomes. This survey confirmed that large numbers of staff were mobilized and that, in most cases, they were able to provide extensive hours of coverage on weekdays. While the predominance of full-time librarians as providers of chat reference may limit the possibilities for expanding service hours in some libraries, those libraries that have more flexible staffing options are in a better position to maintain and improve their coverage. To meet the challenges of sustaining live electronic reference beyond the initial phase of development, managers will need to revisit their staffing plans. Revising workload and job descriptions to recognize the legitimacy of virtual reference activities is a step in the right direction. As a service likely to evolve in response to new patterns of student library consultation, the growth of live electronic reference is unpredictable. However, failure to address staffing implications can only curtail this growth prematurely. Hopefully more comparative research on staffing will lead to the development of effective guidelines in terms of the staff complement needed to sustain growing virtual reference services.

REFERENCES

Coffman, Steve, and Linda Arret. 2004. "To Chat or Not to Chat: Taking Yet Another Look at Virtual Reference, Part 2." *Searcher* 12, no. 8 (September), www.infotoday.com/searcher/sep04/arret_coffman.shtml (accessed October 21, 2004).

Meola, Marc, and Sam Stormont. 2002. *Starting and Operating Live Virtual Reference Services: A How-To-Do-It Manual.* New York: Neal-Schuman.

Reference and User Services Association (RUSA). 2004. "Guidelines for Implementing and Maintaining Virtual Reference Services." *Reference & User Services Quarterly* 44, no. 1 (Fall): 9–13.

Ronan, Jana Smith. 2003. *Chat Reference: A Guide to Virtual Reference Services.* Westport, CT: Libraries Unlimited.

Ronan, Jana Smith, and Carol Turner. 2002. *Chat Reference: SPEC Kit 273.* Washington, DC: Association of Research Libraries.

APPENDIX 4-A

Survey Respondents

Chat reference coordinators from the following Canadian academic libraries participated in the telephone survey on which this paper is based. In order to protect the confidentiality of their responses, there is no explicit identification of these libraries in the text of the paper.

> University of British Columbia Library
> Simon Fraser University Library
> University of Victoria Libraries
> University of Alberta Libraries
> University of Saskatchewan Library
> University of Winnipeg Library
> University of Manitoba Libraries
> University of Western Ontario Libraries
> University of Windsor Library
> University of Toronto Libraries
> University of Guelph Library
> University of Waterloo Library
> York University Libraries
> Ryerson University Library
> Concordia University Libraries
> University of New Brunswick Libraries

PART III

Creating a Reference Future:
Evaluation

Chapter 5

Establishing Performance Targets for a Virtual Reference Service: Counting Totals and Beyond

Deb Hutchison and Michele Pye
With assistance from Susan Huber

OVERVIEW

Live chat reference provides libraries with expanded data about their reference services. Exit survey responses and system-generated statistics help to adjust hours of operation, staffing levels, and more. But few libraries have outlined clear targets for performance. It is possible to establish that questions are increasing or decreasing—but difficult to determine whether success has been achieved. In order to effectively evaluate library services, it is necessary to identify benchmarks, establish realistic targets for performance, and assess success in terms of how well those targets are met. This chapter outlines the process by which researchers at the Vancouver Public Library surveyed chat reference services at similar libraries, used those data to establish benchmarks, and developed performance targets for their virtual reference service.

INTRODUCTION

Most libraries that offer chat reference services are carefully measuring things like the number and types of questions asked, the activity levels for given hours or days, and, of course, patron satisfaction. It is easy to collate data on how many questions were answered last week or last month. It is straightforward to compare today's performance to performance on this day last year. But when exactly are chat reference services successful? The fact is, it is relatively easy to gather data about the questions being answered. It is not so simple to measure success.

Vancouver Public Library (VPL) began offering its first chat reference service, "Find It Now," in May 2003. Six months later, the library launched a similar service, "Homework Help," targeted to school-aged kids. Both services are open Monday to Friday, 4 p.m. to 10 p.m., and are staffed entirely by VPL staff. The library accepts questions of all types from anyone, anywhere. In the first 12 months of service—during which the service was in a pilot phase—over five thousand questions were answered. It felt good. The service seemed busy. Patrons sent wonderful compliments. But, as VPL considered permanently integrating chat reference into its information services, it had to start asking some hard questions.

How many questions does a successful service answer in an hour? What percentage of a library's service population needs to use a service for it to be successful? What is a reasonable cost for chat reference services? With increasing options for service delivery and decreasing budgets, organizations have a responsibility to answer questions like these. By comparing virtual services with benchmarks and performance targets, libraries can assess if and how these services support their goals. As Lankes, Gross, and McClure assert (2003: 402), "library administrators need strong, grounded metrics and commonly understood data to support digital reference services, assess the success of those services, determine resource allocation to services, and determine a means for constant improvement of digital reference within their institutions."

UNDERSTANDING PERFORMANCE TARGETS

Problematically, while the literature makes a strong case for establishing "strong, grounded metrics and commonly understood data" (Lankes, Gross, and McClure, 2003: 402), it offers little guidance in doing so. Publications like *Statistics, Measures and Quality Standards for Assessing Digital Reference Library Services: Guidelines and Procedures* (McClure et al., 2002) provide comprehensive instructions about what to measure and how to measure it, but they stop short of setting targets for these measures. And, while it is reasonable to state that performance targets should be set locally and reflect the unique resources, users, and mandate of each service, practitioners on the front lines have been frustrated by the lack of direction from the literature.

Where the literature has been most useful is in providing a clear description of performance targets. (See, for example, University of Arizona Library; Lankes, Gross and McClure, 2003: 404; and McClure, Lankes, Gross and Choltco-Devlin, 2002: 60–62.) A performance target is clear, measurable, and specific. It represents a level of performance that is both desirable and achievable. It can be derived from benchmarks, but is unique to the goals, objectives, and resources of a particular organization. Significantly, it is distinct from a performance measure: a performance measure might be "total questions asked per hour"; a performance target would be expressed as "the service aims to answer four questions per hour." (Lankes, Gross, and McClure [2003] use the term "quality standard" for the same meaning.)

SETTING PERFORMANCE TARGETS: A MODEL

It was clear that Vancouver Public Library needed a set of agreed-upon performance targets in order to both define and measure the success of its chat reference service. Based on a review of the literature, we established a five-step process for setting performance targets.

1. Select performance measures: answer the question, what are we going to count?

2. Identify the specific data that need to be collected for each measure.
3. Collect benchmark data through a literature review, a survey of peers, and an analysis of the performance of other units in the library.
4. Set challenging yet achievable performance targets, based on the benchmarks.
5. Assess how the library measures up by comparing actual performance to the targets set.

Selecting Measures and Identifying Data

The literature is a rich source of recommended measures and metrics (see Lankes, Gross, and McClure, 2003; McClure et al., 2002; McClure and Lankes, 2001; Marsteller and Neuhaus, 2003). There was thoughtful, comprehensive advice about what to measure and how to measure it—suggestions all libraries should keep in mind if they aim to share and compare their data.

The measures that were selected for this initial exercise were largely quantitative in nature. They included chat questions per capita; chat questions per hour; chat as a proportion of total reference activity; cost per transaction; average transaction time; and repeat usage.

Setting Benchmarks

In establishing benchmarks, we looked to three sources: research reported in the literature; data from similar libraries; and data from other departments within VPL. A number of recent studies (Coffman and Arret, 2004a; Janes, 2003; White, Abels, and Kaske, 2003; Marsteller and Neuhaus, 2003) have begun the process of reporting "industry standards"; these reports are going beyond individual libraries' success stories and instead suggesting means, modes, and medians for chat reference activity.

Benchmarks in the Literature

Steve Coffman and Linda Arret, in their "To Chat or Not To Chat" articles (2004a; 2004b), review suggestive data about the overall performance of chat reference services with particular reference to the quantity of questions received. They report that the Association of Research Libraries' (ARL) 2002 census of virtual reference services showed academic libraries were averaging anywhere from 1 to 14 questions per day (2004a). They also provide data from their own e-mail survey, conducted in October 2003, comparing year-over-year changes in activity. In this latter study, they observed that several respondents were seeing a drop in use and that virtual reference services accounted for a minimal percentage of total reference, even in the most successful services—in short, the performance of virtual services was "generally lacklustre" (2004a). After reviewing their articles, it is easy to feel discouraged about the future of virtual reference services.

Joseph Janes' census of digital reference (2003) also focuses on traffic levels for virtual reference services, looking at data from 162 libraries, reported over three days in November 2003. Janes reports that, on average, survey participants are receiving an average of 11.6 questions per day. Looking at weekdays only, the number is closer to 14.2 questions per day for all library types. Public libraries, accounting for about a quarter of the survey group, seemed to have a slightly higher performance, with an average of 15 questions per day (and presumably a slightly higher number on weekdays).

White, Abels, and Kaske (2003) report that 13 minutes is the average session length for a chat transaction, with a range of three to 29.5 minutes. And Marsteller and Neuhaus (2003) provide some intriguing data about average costs of virtual services, including salary data, as well as overall usage figures and service hours.

Clearly, sources do exist for benchmark-type data. However, a closer look at the survey samples and the data collected raise questions about how relevant these broad numbers should be to local services. These studies tend to include data from libraries of all types and sizes—large and small, academic, special, and public—and often the number of public library respondents is low. Sample sizes also vary widely. Coffman and Arret's e-mail survey, for example, included only a small number of services, few of which involved public libraries (2004a).

Furthermore, the way data are reported can make it challenging to compare chat reference services to one another. For
example, Janes (2003) and Coffman and Arret (2004a) report on
questions per day, although some services operate 24/7 and
others have a more limited schedule. Perhaps it would make
more sense to look at questions per hour of service offered. Likewise, it is perhaps unwise to extrapolate too freely from Janes'
observations of activity during three days in a single month.
Janes himself asks, "Is [8106 questions] a lot? Who knows? [It's
a] good baseline, for further analysis and research" (2003).

The numbers are suggestive, certainly. However, Vancouver
Public Library had to ask how much of this information was re-
flective of and relevant to its particular experience as a large
urban public library. After all, to establish performance targets
that reflect local priorities, it is necessary to be selective about
whose data are used for comparisons. Libraries need to take
care to compare apples to apples: 15 questions per day answered by a statewide consortium serving 12 million users 24/7
means something different than the same number answered by
a single system serving half a million users for six hours a day,
five days a week.

Surveying Peers

The next logical place to obtain benchmarks is from peers. Provided libraries maintain an awareness of their differences, they
can use the performance of their peers to establish workable,
realistic benchmarks. In order to compare apples to apples, it
was necessary to collect data not only about the number of
questions asked via chat, but also about the size of the community served, hours of service, and overall reference activity. Although published data exist in sources such as the (Public
Library Association's (PLA) annual Public Library Data Service
(PLDS) *Statistical Report* (2003), we needed to contact peer libraries for many of the data specific to their chat reference services. As Coffman and Arret point out, "it is difficult to get good
virtual reference statistics. These statistics are not regularly reported to NCES . . . , PLA, ACRL, state libraries, or any other
agencies charged with gathering library statistics" (2004a).

Table 5-1
Participating Libraries

Cleveland Public Library	Multnomah County Library
Baltimore County Public Library (responded as Maryland AskUsNow)	Orange County Library Public Library of Charlotte & Mecklenburg County
Denver Public Library	San Jose Public Library
Enoch Pratt Free Library	Seattle Public Library
King County Library System	Sno-Isle Public Library
Montgomery County Public Libraries (responded as Maryland AskUsNow)	Toronto Public Library Vancouver Public Library

Vancouver Public Library is a large, urban public library serving an immediate population of approximately 578,000. It has a central branch and 21 branches. To identify VPL's peers, we used PLA's 2003 PLDS data to identify public libraries meeting three criteria: a minimum legal service-area population of 500,000; at least 15 branches; and a materials budget of $3 million or more. They cross-referenced the short list with the Washington State Library's list of chat reference services to identify a total of 20 large, urban, North American public libraries offering chat reference services. This formed the sample for the study.

Fourteen libraries provided data for the survey (see Table 5-1 for a list of respondents). Several respondents indicated they were part of a consortium, while a number of others provide chat reference independently (two libraries contributed consortium-wide data rather than individual figures). A few services use after-hours contract services to cover certain hours of service. The majority of the services that responded have elected to offer full reference services via chat; the remainder consider themselves to be triage services.

Internal Sources for Benchmarks

Internal peers are one last, but important, source for benchmark data. Chat reference services at Vancouver Public Library are coordinated through the Virtual Library department, which operates in some ways like a virtual branch. Therefore, it is possible to look also to the performance of other branches in the system to establish targets for chat services. This is especially useful for difficult-to-find external data, such as costs.

SETTING PERFORMANCE TARGETS AND MEASURING SUCCESS

With the five-step model for setting performance targets in hand, we began to analyze data about chat service usage and activity collected from VPL's peers and internal departments (Table 5-2 illustrates an example of the process). We looked in particular at both average (mean) and median performance, as well as at the overall range of performance. In establishing each target, the library considered its priorities and the mandate of its chat service and selected what it felt was an achievable, yet challenging, goal.

One issue that became clear during the analysis of the peer survey data was that individual libraries are not all counting the same things: in particular, some libraries count questions while others count transactions or sessions. For the purposes of this report, we chose to collapse the two (and call them "questions"), but clearly this needs to be addressed in the future.

Table 5-2
Setting Performance Targets: Sample Grid

Select performance measure	Identify needed data	Collect benchmark data	Set performance target	Compare actual performance to target
Chat questions per capita	Total questions per year	Average:	In the year ____, we aim to answer 1 question for	Performance: 1 question / ____ users.
	– – – – – Population of service area	Median: High:	every ____ users in our service area	Target MET / NOT MET
...	...	...	...	...
...	...	...	...	...

Chat Questions per Capita

In assessing the quantity of questions received via chat, it is significant to consider the population of the service area. After all, population varies considerably among systems. A given number of questions generated by a population of 500,000 should have more weight than the same number of questions generated by a population of 5,000,000. All participating libraries provided data for this measure. Population data were drawn largely from the 2003 PLDS *Statistical Report*, although in a few cases in which the service area for chat differed from the local service area, the researchers relied on self-reported data. Numbers of questions received for January through August 2004 were reported by surveyed libraries; the researchers then annualized the data provided in order to have an annual per capita figure.

On average, chat services received one question for every 239 individuals served (almost double the 2003 data); the median was one question for every 189 individuals served. Cleveland Public Library ranked highest, answering one question for every 44 users in 2004.[1]

Based on these data, Vancouver Public Library set a target of answering, on an annual basis, one question for every one hundred individuals in its service area. While this number isn't quite at the level of best-of-breed, it seemed to be well above the average and appropriate for a relatively young service. Based on annualized data for 2004, VPL ranks third among its peers, answering one question for every 98 users. Therefore, VPL is meeting its target.

Chat Questions per Hour

Just as population needs to be taken into account when evaluating the overall use of a service, so it is important to consider hours of service. Eight of the survey respondents offer 24/7 chat reference, while the rest offer regular scheduled service hours— typically 30–50 per week. By considering the total number of questions received along with total service hours, it is possible to get a measure of the efficiency of the service: clearly, answering

20 questions in a 4-hour service period differs from answering 20 questions in a 24-hour period.

Data for this measure were self-reported: both hours of service per week and total questions answered. All respondents provided data for this measure. The analysis is based on total questions asked from January through August 2004, divided by total hours of service offered. What has not been considered is how many staff cover each hour of service (e.g., one hour of service may reflect two or more staff hours at some services).

On average, the services surveyed received 1.6 questions per hour, with a median of 0.9 questions per hour. Maryland AskUsNow reported the highest overall activity levels, with 4.8 questions asked per hour of service; the lowest was 0.1 questions/hour.

Looking at these data, VPL set an initial target of 3.5 questions per hour—again, better than the average, but not quite best-of-breed. Based on performance in 2004, which shows that VPL ranks third among its peers and answers 3.8 questions per hour of service, it can be stated that VPL is performing strongly in this measure.

However, for this measure it seemed that a key measure was to look at activity levels for VPL's chat reference service in comparison to other internal departments, as well as to external peers. Since chat services are analogous to branch information services, we compared chat activity to activity at other branches. Using data on reference questions only (excluding directional questions) for the first six months of 2004, we determined that, on average, VPL branches answer 7.9 questions per hour of service, with a median of 7.6 questions per hour. For the same period, VPL's chat reference service averaged 4.7 reference questions per hour—placing it 18th out of 21 branches.

In consideration of this internal benchmarking, the performance target was revised upward from 3.5 questions per hour to 7.5 questions per hour. This is ambitious, since it will require nearly doubling current activity levels. Also, since VPL currently staffs its chat service with two staff members, it is likely that staff will have to work almost at capacity at all times. However, if VPL intends to establish its electronic services and resources as a virtual branch, expectations for the chat service should be on a par with internal peers.

Chat versus Total Reference Activity

A third area was how chat stacked up as a proportion of total reference activity. It is important to consider chat services in the context of all information services. Coffman and Arret (2004a) frequently comment that chat services, no matter how busy, account for only a very small percentage of overall activity. We wanted to investigate further to see how VPL performed in this area.

To analyze data for this measure, we annualized self-reported counts of total chat questions for January through August 2004, and calculated each as a percentage of total reference transactions, as reported in the 2003 *PLDS Statistical Report*. Both data sets include all types of questions: reference, specific item, and directional.

On average, chat reference accounts for 0.6% of total reference activity for 2004 among the survey group. The median is lower still, 0.3%, and most services reported numbers below 0.5%. The best performance in this measure is from Cleveland, where chat reference accounts for 3.3% of total reference for 2004.

For this measure, VPL set two targets: one short term, and one longer term. The first target is to account for 0.42% of total reference. We nicknamed this the "bang-for-your-buck factor," since the budget for staffing and software accounts for 0.42% of the library's total operating budget. Longer term, the hope is to increase this number to about 1.0%, which is roughly comparable to e-mail reference at VPL. Since VPL's chat service accounts for 0.4% of total reference (ranking it fifth overall), it appeared that the first target is achievable, and the second is a good goal for the future.

As a secondary analysis, we also asked participating libraries to share their data about e-mail reference. They subjected these data to similar analysis and learned that the numbers are not significantly different—despite the difference in scrutiny being applied to each. On average, e-mail accounted for 0.5% of total reference for 2004, slightly lower than chat. The median, 0.3%, is identical to that for chat services. VPL saw the highest overall proportion of e-mail, at 1.0%.

Costs

An area that we were eager to explore was the cost of chat services. It is generally agreed that costs of reference services are extremely difficult to measure (for an excellent discussion of this, see Marsteller and Ware, 2003). Furthermore, libraries tend to be reluctant to air what may potentially be "dirty laundry" in public. Consequently, there is very little specific information about the costs of chat reference services available. At the same time, all libraries would agree that it is important to consider the costs and benefits of chat services to be certain that limited resources are allocated appropriately.

The first step was to survey VPL's large urban public library peers. Fewer than half reported any data for this measure, and only two (including VPL) reported specific staff costs as well as software costs. These data were insufficient to serve as the basis for benchmarks. Instead, the researchers turned again to internal peers: to the other branches in the VPL system. An internal study, carried out over three months from December 2003 to February 2004, looked at the total staff cost per reference question answered. This cost per transaction approach is generally considered to be one of the most blunt measures (Marsteller and Ware, 2003), but at least it gave the researchers a starting place. In order to prevent results that favored services answering large quantities of directional questions, only reference questions were analyzed.

Over the three months of the study, Vancouver Public Library's branches reported an average cost per question of $2.89 (USD); the median was slightly higher at $3.58. In the same period, the Central Library reported an average of $3.04 per question and a median of $3.35. The average cost per reference question for chat reference during the same timeframe was $7.09. While this number seemed high (VPL ranked 19th of 21 branches), the researchers were cheered that the early costs of nearly $11.00 per question had come down considerably.

Although VPL's chat service outperformed a few of the smaller branches and subject divisions, its overall costs were still high compared to systemwide averages. As a result, the library selected a performance target for this measure of $4.50 per reference question. This would still put the chat service's costs above average, but would put it on a par with several VPL branches. In order to meet this target, VPL will need to review staff and software costs to assess possible efficiencies.

Transaction Time and Capacity

Assessing average transaction time gives libraries another tool they can use to evaluate chat services. While the length of a transaction is not immediately translatable into a measure of the quality or usage of a service (though longer transaction times tend to reflect more complex questions), this information can be used to assess the capacity of a service. In other words, knowing the average transaction length will help libraries to determine how many questions can reasonably be answered by one staff member in a given period of time. In turn, this can help libraries to establish reasonable targets (or minimums and maximums) for total questions per hour. By setting targets for this measure, libraries can aim to increase their efficiency in responding to questions. In the future, libraries could also use this measure to compare chat reference to other modes of reference, such as face-to-face.

Nine respondents provided data for this measure. All indicated the times were per transaction, not per question asked. Many used their transcripts and logs to collect these data; others relied on anecdote. On average, services reported they spent 13.3 minutes on each transaction; the median was slightly lower at 13 minutes per transaction. With an average of nearly 18 minutes per transaction, VPL ranked eighth overall and definitely short of the average.

Anecdotal evidence indicated that the majority of Vancouver Public Library's questions were research reference questions, requiring substantial reference interviews and instruction in the use of resources, so the performance target was set slightly below the norm, at 15 minutes per transaction. VPL feels that its staff, as they gain more experience and receive additional training, will be able to increase their efficiency to this level without negatively affecting the quality of the transaction.

Repeat Users

The final measure was repeat usage. Working on the assumption that patrons return if they are happy with the service they have received in the past, we concluded that repeat usage could be understood as an indicator of patron satisfaction. (It is worth considering that some repeat usage can probably be accounted for by patrons with technical problems returning more than once.)

Sources of data for repeat usage were varied. Seven respondents shared data based on exit surveys, anecdotal evidence, and log analysis. Periods of time analyzed also varied widely, from six months up.

On average, 35% of questions or transactions were initiated by repeat users. The highest numbers—57 percent—were reported by King County. Based on the data and on the fact that its Homework Help service draws many repeat users, VPL established a performance target of 40 percent. When VPL's chat reference logs were analyzed, the library ranked second with repeat usage of 48%, exceeding its target.

DID VANCOUVER PUBLIC LIBRARY MEASURE UP?

In assessing performance against its benchmark-driven targets, Vancouver Public Library's chat services met or exceeded over half of their performance targets (see Table 5-3 for a summary). There is still work to be done, however, to bring down costs per transaction, reduce average transaction times, increase the proportion of chat questions in overall reference activity, and generally increase use of chat services. In some cases, VPL has set some very challenging targets.

Going forward, the library intends to focus on two areas to meet these targets: marketing and staff training. Increased marketing, both locally and province-wide, will drive additional traffic to VPL's chat services. The library will also implement formal, ongoing staff training in key areas, including online subject resources, troubleshooting, and instructional techniques. Some staff find chat reference a new and challenging, even intimidating, medium to work in. As staff continue to gain experience and build confidence, the library will be able to provide better service in shorter times.

Table 5-3
How Did VPL Measure Up?

Measure	Benchmark data source	Benchmarks	Target	Actual per- formance	Met/ not met
Chat questions per capita	External	Average: 1:239 Median: 1:189 High: 1:44 Low: 1:1348	1:100	1:98	Met
Chat questions per hour	External	Average: 1.6 Median: 0.9 High: 4.8 Low: 0.1	3.5	3.8	Met
	Internal	Average: 7.9 Median: 7.6 High: 16 Low: 4.2	7.5	4.7	Not met
Chat vs. total reference activity	External	Average: 0.6% Median: 0.3% High: 3.3% Low: 0.1%	0.4–1.0%	0.4%	Met
Cost per transaction	Internal	Average: $2.89 Median: $3.58 High: $7.47 Low: $1.46	$4.50	$7.09	Not met
Transaction time	External	Average: 13.3 mins Median: 13 mins High: 18 mins Low: 8 mins	15 mins	18 mins	Not met
Repeat users	External	Average: 35% Median: 36% High: 57% Low: 10%	40%	48%	Met

In the future, the researchers would like to reassess Vancouver Public Library's performance vis-à-vis the targets that were set for this study. It would also be valuable to contact the participants in this study for a further year's worth of data, and to reassess benchmarks and possibly reset targets accordingly. An institution-wide review of reference services is now underway at VPL, so it is especially fitting that the researchers were taking a hard look at one mode of reference service and developing a model that can be transferred easily to other modes.

FUTURE TARGETS

The measures investigated so far are largely quantitative. While the data the researchers have collected will aid VPL in improving the efficiency and productivity of its service, the researchers would like to look more closely at the quality of responses and at other "soft" aspects of the service. The researchers believe that their five-step model can be applied in these other areas.

Areas for future research include staff courtesy and friendliness, as well as accuracy and completeness of responses. In addition to analyzing VPL's own transcripts for these data, the researchers would like to work with services at similar libraries to develop benchmarks for these qualitative measures, too. Research questions might include, "How many questions should we answer correctly and completely to be a "successful" service?" The researchers would also like to analyze VPL's market penetration and set targets for reaching local schools, for example.

LESSONS LEARNED

Before the researchers set out to do this study, they asked many of their colleagues in other organizations questions like, "How do you measure success?" "How do you know when you have achieved success?" "How do you explain success to your stakeholders?" They learned quickly that most libraries were in the same boat. Virtual services were built in response to a general sense of shifting user needs and a genuine desire to serve users better. Then libraries waited to see what would happen. Finally, with a year or two of experience and perspective under their belts, libraries were ready to step back and look at all the data that have been collected and start to ask, "But what does it mean?"

Using the five-step process for setting performance targets enabled Vancouver Public Library to articulate both the successes of and ongoing challenges for its chat reference services.

By methodically moving through the process of selecting performance measures, identifying and collecting data for benchmarking, setting targets for performance, and finally comparing actual performance to those targets, VPL was able to clearly define success for its stakeholders, and to do so in a manner that reflected its unique community, resources, and mandate.

Virtual reference is under a microscope; that much is clear. Critics of chat reference services are beginning to find and distribute dire statistics about sub-par performance. If proponents of chat reference are to argue for the ongoing support of these services, it is necessary to have clear, articulated, measurable standards for success with a basis in meaningful, relevant benchmarks. As painful as it can be at times, this is a healthy and necessary exercise. And libraries would do well to apply the same microscope to all forms of reference.

NOTE

1. In seeking to establish benchmarks, the researchers were interested primarily in overall averages and front-runners. The averages are useful in identifying a standard baseline for performance; the front-runners inspire goals to aim for. As a result, means, medians, and ranges are published rather than all of the specific data reported by individual libraries. Detailed data have been shared with all participating libraries and are available to others upon request.

REFERENCES

Coffman, Steve, and Linda Arret. 2004a. "To Chat or Not to Chat—Taking Another Look at Virtual Reference, Part 1." *Information Today* 12, no. 7, www.infotoday.com/searcher/jul04/arret_coffman.shtml (accessed October 27, 2004).

Coffman, Steve, and Linda Arret. 2004b. "To Chat or Not to Chat—Taking Yet Another Look at Virtual Reference, Part 2." *Information Today* 12, no. 8, www.infotoday.com/searcher/sep04/arret_coffman.shtml (accessed October 27, 2004).

Janes, Joseph. 2003. "The Global Census of Digital Reference." Presentation at the Virtual Reference Desk 2003 Digital Reference Conference, "The Reference Roundup" (November), San Antonio, TX, www.vrd2003.org/proceedings/presentation.cfm?PID=162 (accessed September 29, 2004).

Lankes, R. David, Melissa Gross, and Charles R. McClure. 2003. "Cost, Statistics, Measures and Standards for Digital Reference Services: A Preliminary View." *Library Trends* 51, no. 3: 401–413.

Marsteller, Matthew R., and Paul Neuhaus. 2003. "Providing Chat Reference Service: A Survey of Current Practices." In *Implementing Digital Reference Services: Setting Standards and Making it Real*, edited by R. David Lankes, Charles R. McClure, Melissa Gross, and Jeffrey Pomerantz (pp. 61–74). London: Facet.

Marsteller, Matthew, and Susan Ware. 2003. "Models for Measuring and Evaluating Reference Costs: A Comparative Analysis of Traditional and Virtual Reference Services" (November). Presentation at the Virtual Reference Desk 2003 Digital Reference Conference, "The Reference Roundup," San Antonio, TX, www.vrd2003.org/proceedings/presentation.cfm?PID=255 (accessed February 2, 2004).

McClure, Charles R., R. David Lankes, Melissa Gross, and Beverly Choltco-Devlin. 2002. *Statistics, Measures and Quality Standards for Assessing Digital Reference Library Services: Guidelines and Procedures: Draft*. Syracuse, NY: Information Institute of Syracuse, Syracuse University, http://quartz.syr.edu/quality/Quality.pdf (accessed February 5, 2004).

McClure, Charles R., and R. David Lankes. 2001. *Assessing Quality in Digital Reference Services: A Prospectus: Draft*. Syracuse, NY: Information Institute of Syracuse, Syracuse University, http://quartz.syr.edu/quality/Overview.htm (accessed September 23, 2003).

Public Library Data Service. 2003. *Statistical Report 2003*. Chicago: Public Library Association.

University of Arizona Library, Strategic Long Range Planning Team. n.d. "Performance Measures," www.library.arizona.edu/library/teams/slrp/syllabus/measure.html (accessed February 5, 2004).

"Virtual Reference Services Sites Grid." n.d. http://66.212.65.207/textdocs/vrsgrid.htm (accessed February 15, 2004).

White, Marilyn Domas, Eileen G. Abels, and Neal Kaske. 2003. "Evaluation of Chat Reference Service Quality: Pilot Study." *D-Lib Magazine* 9, no. 2 (February), www.dlib.org/dlib/february03/white/02white.html (accessed June 24, 2003).

Chapter 6

Creating the Infrastructure for Digital Reference Research: Examining the Digital Reference Electronic Warehouse (DREW) Project

Scott Nicholson and R. David Lankes

OVERVIEW

There are hundreds of digital reference services generating knowledge through human intermediation every day; however, the lack of a schema for archiving reference transactions from multiple services makes it difficult to create a shared database of transactions for digital reference research. Such a schema would also allow researchers to develop tools that practitioners can employ; this will create a collaborative environment for digital reference evaluation. The goal of this work is to outline the steps needed to develop this schema, present the results of a survey of digital reference services, explore some of the pitfalls in the process, and envision the future uses of this Digital Reference Electronic Warehouse (DREW).

INTRODUCTION

There are hundreds of digital reference services around the world providing answers and resources in response to user needs. If collected into a knowledge base, it would be useful for researchers in exploring this process. Information-seeking research has been an active line of exploration for decades, and there are many theories developed from small samples that could be explored with this larger data set. In addition, by examining the common works referred to in different types of questions, automatically generated directories of high-quality material could be created and shared. The goal of the DREW project is to create a large database of reference transactions so researchers can better understand the process and to create tools for measurement and evaluation that managers of reference services can employ.

OTHER DIGITAL REFERENCE ARCHIVES

Most reference services maintain some type of archive. That archive may be accessible only to the administrators, it may be a useful archive for those answering questions, or it may be available to users of the system. A number of projects, such as Ask-A-Scientist (www.madsci.org/) and Google Answers (www.answers.google.com/answers), allow anyone to search the project's internal archives of question/answer pairs. While this is useful, it lacks the richness available if the transactions were collected by multiple services. One of the largest shared archives of reference transactions is QuestionPoint's Knowledge-Base (OCLC, 2004). Use of QuestionPoint's Knowledge Base is limited to those institutions participating in the QuestionPoint service, which allows for collaborative reference work. The Knowledge Base consists of human-edited and selected questions with nonduplicated transactions to aid information seekers.

One goal of the DREW project is to maintain a relationship with other major reference archives, such as QuestionPoint. Examining these similar projects allows us to determine the needs of DREW and learn from the exploration of others. DREW, being a project to provide data for researchers about the process, requires a different type of warehouse. The transactions will not be edited for content, although personally identifiable information will be removed. Transactions on the same topic are desired as that will allow the discovery of trends and changes over time. Therefore, DREW will complement these other archives and knowledge bases.

The current goal of DREW is to create a schema that is compatible with different existing knowledge base projects. The challenge of this project is overcoming the complexity of many different services and user types. The landscape of digital reference is one of many types of services, librarians, and users interacting with a similar base of resources. There will be patterns across services, although teasing them out of the complex data is a challenge. The authors turn to complexity theory as the theoretical support for the success of this project.

COMPLEXITY THEORY AND DREW

To date, knowledge-base work in digital reference has been primarily a deductive process. That is, either a service makes every transaction searchable, or go through an extensive transformation process of question selection, editing, and incorporation into a pre-determined subject hierarchy. These deductive, and largely manual, processes have obvious scale problems. Other issues in the deductive construction of knowledge bases are

- *Context dependencies:* Information in knowledge bases is very context dependent. It is quite possible that the only application of the information in a digital reference transcript is to that particular interchange between librarian and patron.
- *Metadata creation:* Time, labor, and money are involved in creating metadata for transcripts and digital reference interchanges so that they can be later discovered and retrieved by end users. While some of this effort may be part of the reference process itself (for example, classifying a question for distribution in QuestionPoint), it may still require effort to confirm and refine this classification data for inclusion in a knowledge base.

- *Chunking:* It is well known that users will ask several questions in both real-time and asynchronous transactions. How those questions and answers are "broken apart" is often dependent on human intervention and a great deal of interpretation.
- *Fact shifting and temporal dependencies:* Answers to reference questions are often time dependent. From the name of the U.S. President to the height of Mount Everest, answers to even simple questions change. These changes, while concrete, are often hard to track over time. This does not even take into account "grey" areas where an answer or fact to apply to a question is a matter of choice among equally good options.

While the use of full-text approaches such as vector-based information retrieval may mitigate some of these problems, they do not solve core difficulties of fact shifting, nor do they take into account the dynamic nature of the information presented. While the knowledge base grows, the relationship between information may change as well. This situation is complicated when archives from different services are combined.

We argue that attempting to devise, scale, and equip a deductive approach to knowledge bases is ultimately unworkable. Furthermore, it is time to try a radically different, inductive approach. Simply put: let the knowledge base, or more specifically, the agents representing digital reference output, organize themselves.

COMPLEX ADAPTIVE SYSTEMS

The inductive approach proposed in this prospective is grounded in complexity theory and, more specifically, the concept of complex adaptive systems as conceptualized by Holland (1995). This chapter does not explain the whole of complexity theory or delve any further than an operational explanation of complex adaptive systems in this document. For a deeper understanding of complexity theory see Waldrop (1992); for complex adaptive systems see Holland (1995); and for the application of complexity to digital reference see Lankes (1998).

Put simply, complex adaptive systems are grounded in the creation of autonomous agents that self-organize based on relatively simple rules. This organization is emergent in that it is not the product of some predetermined course, but a result of the interactions of the agents themselves. The most common analogy is that of flocking birds. Systems to simulate the flocking behavior of birds are effectively replicated by creating independent agents in a virtual space with a set of very simple rules like "you must move forward: get as close as you can to those agents near you; do not hit anything." Such simulations demonstrate very effectively that such systems produce complex results with swarms of birds on a screen avoiding obstacles . . . even though they were never programmed to do obstacle avoidance . . . or swarming.

Models using these principles have also effectively been created to simulate the activities of financial markets, traffic flows, and population studies. The point is, complex adaptive systems, consisting of the interactions of autonomous agents, have been effectively used to create systems impossible to create in a deductive manner, which would require thousands of rules and lines of code to anticipate every possible contingency. Already artificial intelligence systems have moved away from these so-called frame-based and expert system approaches toward neural nets and inductive simulations.

These systems are also dynamic in that the agents constantly adapt to a changing environment. They constantly seek an optimal state in changing conditions. So the virtual birds will avoid obstacles in new ways as new obstacles are added. In simulations of biological systems, agents will adapt to changes in weather or food supply. It is this dynamism that makes an inductive approach particularly suitable to digital reference knowledge bases.

In order to examine the contents of DREW and develop new, inductive approaches to knowledge-base analysis and construction, the research team must first define the autonomous agents in the complex knowledge-base environment. These agents, according to Holland (1995), must have three mechanisms:

- *Tags:* Mechanisms that agents utilize for aggregation and flows of information

- *Internal models:* A representation of the environment used by an agent to anticipate and adapt to the environment
- *Building blocks:* Components of internal models combined to build, test, and rebuild internal models.

The "internal models," and "building blocks" will be the result of future research. Tagging, or the mechanisms used for information flow and identification, however, are central to the present study. These tags can be thought of fields, or metadata elements. By identifying common fields in digital reference transactions (knowledge-base agents) these agents can be compared, clustered, and examined.

DETERMINING THE FIELDS

The first step in creating a data warehouse is to determine the fields that will be collected. As there are many different digital reference services, any schema for capturing information from these different services will result in compromises. In order to better understand what fields would be appropriate to capture, a survey was taken of digital reference service representatives with the goal of learning what fields services currently collect, or are willing to collect, in regard to the patron, question, answer, and expert. The survey also gathered demographic information, such as the communication methods used for question acceptance and question resolution, number of questions received per month, platform used, and consortia information.

DEMOGRAPHICS OF RESPONDENTS

There were 53 responses to the survey, and there was little duplication by members of the same consortial group in the survey responses. Of those services that could be affiliated with an institution, slightly more than half (53%) were from academic libraries. The remaining services were fairly evenly split between public (15%), special and other libraries (17%) and AskA services without a specific library affiliation (14%). About half (47%) of the responses were from chat-based services, 38% were from Web-based asynchronous services, and the remaining 15% used

Table 6-1
Percentage of Respondents Using Each Reference Tool (N=53)

Platform/Software	Percentage of Respondents
(E-mail, Web form, or in-house tool combined)	27%
Question Point	23%
Tutor.com	21%
E-mail	13%
24/7	8%
Web form + e-mail	8%
In-house tool	6%
Altarama RefTracker	4%
QABuilder 2.0	4%
Docutek VRL Plus	2%
eAssist NetAgent	2%
ExpertCity's Desktopstreaming	2%
LivePerson (HumanClick)	2%
Open Ask A Question	2%
PHP Live Support	2%

e-mail or another communication platform for reference. The median number of Web-form-based questions was 80 per month, and the median number of chat questions was 120 per month. Another demographic collected was the platform used by the reference service. The results after cleaning the data are in Table 6-1. The entries for e-mail, Web form + e-mail, and in-house tool may refer to the same type of service—some type of system using existing e-mail and Web servers. If these are combined, then there are three clear popular choices—Question Point, Tutor.com, and some type of in-house use of existing resources.

EXPLORATION OF COMMUNICATION FORMS

A series of questions on the survey sought information about the communication practices of different service types. For example, all surveyed e-mail and Web-form-based services e-mailed

Table 6-2
Formats of Final Resolution of Reference Transactions (N=53)

Incoming question format	E-mail answer	Web-form answer	Chat answer	Other form (telephone, visit)
E-mail	98%	0%	1%	1%
Web form	23%	74%	0%	3%
Chat	7%	3%	80%	10%

a copy of the answer or transaction to the patron; however, only 72% of the chat-based services regularly sent a copy of the transaction to the user.

A similar set of questions explored the format through which questions are eventually resolved. These results, in Table 6-2, show that there is not much crossover between formats. Chat reference is resolved in chat about 80% of the time, and Web-form questions are resolved via Web-forms or e-mail most of the time. The high percentage of other forms of answers that started as chat reference is probably because the synchronous connection has already been made, and it is then convenient to complete the transaction via phone.

FIELDS COLLECTED BY SERVICES

In order to understand what information services are collecting, the analysis is presented in two parts. First, the fields currently collected by services are presented. Following that, the discussion turns to the data that inform the rest of this schema: what fields are services either currently collecting or willing to collect?

Table 6-3 lists the fields, sorted by category and overall usage, of what services currently collect during the reference process. Looking at the overall results, the most common set of fields currently collected about a reference transaction are patron e-mail and name; question text, date, and time; and the response text, date, and time. This aggregate set of fields disguises patterns that appear when the results are broken out by communication method used.

Table 6-3
Percentage of Services Currently Collecting Specified Fields
(N=53)

	Overall	Web form	Chat	E-mail/other
Patron information				
E-mail	77%	90%	68%	67%
Name	72%	80%	68%	50%
Country	36%	65%	20%	0%
State	34%	55%	24%	0%
Member of organization	34%	35%	32%	17%
City	32%	55%	20%	17%
Educational level	30%	40%	28%	0%
Phone number	23%	25%	16%	17%
Professional role	23%	30%	16%	0%
Question information				
Text of question	93%	100%	88%	83%
Date	91%	95%	92%	67%
Time	85%	85%	92%	50%
Routing/Referral information	45%	30%	60%	17%
Subject (free-text)	43%	35%	44%	83%
Deadline for answer	17%	30%	4%	17%
Desired form of answer	11%	10%	8%	17%
Purpose	9%	20%	4%	0%
Previously consulted resources	9%	10%	8%	0%
Subject (from a list)	8%	10%	8%	0%
Responder information				
Name	53%	50%	60%	33%
E-mail	45%	35%	52%	50%
Institution	45%	45%	52%	0%
State	34%	40%	32%	0%
Country	32%	40%	28%	0%
City	28%	35%	28%	0%
Title	25%	30%	24%	0%
Telephone	17%	20%	16%	0%
Qualifications	17%	20%	16%	17%

(Continued)

Table 6-3
Percentage of Services Currently Collecting Specified Fields
(N=53) (*Continued*)

	Overall	Web form	Chat	E-mail/other
Response information				
Date	93%	90%	96%	83%
Text of response	89%	95%	88%	67%
Time	87%	80%	96%	67%
Resources consulted	51%	65%	40%	33%

Since the two common communication methods are Web form and chat, they will be examined individually. Chat services tend to be more free-form, and therefore may not explicitly collect many fields. Some services ask the user to set up an account before the chat session; this will result in more information about the patron, but not more information about the specific information need behind a reference transaction. Even though chat services tended to collect less information than average, many still collect the patron name and e-mail; question text, date, time, and referral/routing information; and the response text, date, and time. One field of note here is the above-average collection of referral/routing information. Many chat services reported capturing fields like IP address, which was the most common information put into the "Other" open-ended survey questions. In addition, as seen earlier, chat sessions end in a different communication channel 20% of the time; they therefore have a stronger need to capture this type of transferal information.

The group of Web-form reference services captured more information on average than other types of services; this is not surprising as the process of asking a question via a Web-based form is more structured than asking the same question via e-mail or chat. The most common fields currently collected via Web-form-based asynchronous reference are patron e-mail, name, country, and state; question text, date, and time; response text, date, time, and responses collected. Since the information is collected in small fielded pieces, it is then easier to keep those pieces in a data warehouse. It is because of this that DREW will start by aggregating Web-form-based services, and then move to more free-form services as the warehouse develops.

One interesting pattern is the lack of information collected about the person answering the question during the process. There are two types of individuals who answer questions— those who are trained to do research and answer a question from existing resources (such as librarians) and those who are able to answer questions in a specific topic area because they are trained experts in that area. Librarians are trained to provide citation information and to document the authoritativeness of an answer through the support of external works. Experts, on the other hand, provide the authority for their answer based upon their credentials. If services do not keep information about the person who answered the question, then the authority behind an expert-answered question disappears. Because of this, it is important to encourage experts who are answering questions to supply references to works that would contain the answer to the question, even when they know the answer without looking anything up. As these experts may not have been trained as librarians, the administrator of the system needs to ensure that training is available in the basics of creating a response that will have supported authority without the identity of the answerer.

FIELDS THAT SERVICES ARE WILLING TO COLLECT

Another way of looking at the data is to explore which fields services either collect now or are willing to collect in the future. The data was recalculated using this new model, and the results are in Table 6-4. This is important in aiding the development of the DREW schema. While services may not currently be collecting information, they may be more willing to collect the information if they perceive that the data will be useful in improving their service and the understanding of the field. While those doing chat reference currently collect the least amount of information, they were the most willing to collect additional information for this research. Conversely, the Web-form services were less willing to collect additional fields.

Looking at the Overall column, one can see that services are willing to collect much more information than they currently

Table 6-4
Percentage of Services Currently Collecting or Willing to Collect Specified Fields (N=53)

	Overall	Web form	Chat	E-mail/other
Patron information				
E-mail	83%	90%	80%	67%
Name	79%	85%	76%	67%
State	70%	75%	64%	67%
Member of organization	70%	65%	72%	67%
City	68%	75%	60%	83%
Country	66%	80%	52%	67%
Phone number	59%	65%	52%	50%
Educational level	59%	55%	64%	50%
Professional role	49%	45%	48%	50%
Question information				
Text of question	100%	100%	100%	100%
Date	100%	100%	100%	100%
Time	94%	90%	100%	83%
Routing/Referral information	83%	75%	92%	67%
Subject (free-text)	76%	60%	80%	100%
Deadline for answer	72%	75%	64%	83%
Previously consulted resources	70%	75%	64%	67%
Desired form of answer	59%	60%	52%	67%
Subject (from a list)	51%	45%	52%	50%
Purpose	51%	55%	48%	50%
Responder information				
Name	79%	75%	88%	50%
Institution	79%	70%	92%	50%
E-mail	70%	60%	80%	50%
State	64%	55%	72%	50%
Country	62%	55%	68%	50%
Title	62%	55%	72%	50%
City	59%	50%	68%	50%
Qualifications	53%	45%	60%	50%
Telephone	51%	45%	60%	33%

(Continued)

Table 6-4
Percentage of Services Currently Collecting or Willing to Collect Specified Fields (N=53) (*Continued*)

	Overall	Web form	Chat	E-mail/other
Response information				
Text of response	98%	100%	100%	83%
Date	98%	95%	100%	100%
Time	94%	90%	100%	83%
Resources consulted	77%	80%	76%	67%

collect. One obstacle is the fact that patrons are less likely to ask a question if they have to fill out more fields. The patron and expert information need be collected only once, then matched to each question through a logon process. The question and response information would need to be gathered every time.

DEVELOPING THE DREW SCHEMA

In order to develop the proposed DREW schema, we will now explore each area of the survey and discuss the usefulness of the fields to research needs. There are two types of research needs that are important: the needs of administrators in understanding their own digital reference system, and the needs of researchers in looking at the larger-scale picture.

Transaction Information

One of the challenges of DREW is that it will hold different forms of intermediation. The goal is to collect questions from all types of digital reference services—chat, e-mail, form-based, and so on. Therefore, at the center of the DREW record will be the information from the transaction. For a chat transaction, the body of the chat will be included. In an e-mail transaction where there was little restriction on the information in the e-mail, the e-mail text will be included. If a Web form was used to collect fielded information, then the question and response will be divided and included. There will also be a field to identify the type of transactional data in the record. A priority for researchers is to develop algorithms that will divide the large textual chat and e-mail transcripts into separate questions and answers.

Patron Information

Even though services are willing to collect considerable patron information, little of this is actually needed or even desired in understanding the question-answering process. One of the common fields that was a write-in on the survey was *Zip Code*; this field combines city and state information and can be used to map DREW to a demographic database, but does not intrude upon the personally identifiable information about the patron. Another useful field for DREW is the intended *Educational Level* of the transaction.

Question Information

It is more important to collect information about the question than information about the patron, as seen with the educational level field above. Fields such as *Date, Time,* and *Previously Consulted Sources* are all potentially useful. Some type of *Free-Text Subject* and *Category* information is also useful, and one of the areas of research is to attempt to automatically map this to a common list. Services are willing to share *Referral Information*; the key information for DREW is if the question was answered by the service that received it or if a *Referral Service* was involved.

Responder Information

As before, services are the least willing to collect information about the person answering the question. QuestionPoint actively removes this information (P. Rumbaugh, personal communication, July 6, 2004). One field about the expert would be useful: *Responder Role*, which will identify the responder as a content expert who answers the question from experience or an information professional who found the answer in another source.

Response Information

All four fields listed on the survey are useful for research and many services are willing to collect them; therefore Response Date, Response Time, and Response Resources are all part of this proposed schema. The field Response Type (based on the NETREF standard [Library of Congress, 2004]) can identify the type of response (Answer, Clarification, Out of Scope, Other).

CURRENT CHALLENGES

There are three current research challenges for this project: NISO standards and threading, subject-list authority, and privacy.

NISO Standards and Threading

One goal of this process is to create a schema for archiving that is compatible with the networked reference services protocol NISO AZ, a.k.a. NetRef (Library of Congress, 2004). In its current configuration, this standard is designed to assist with the operational needs of passing questions from one service to another. The DREW schema is designed to be applied to the transaction after it is completed. It is important, therefore, that the archival schema be compatible with the operational standard.

One significant issue in the transition from the operational standard to archival form is the de-threading and cleaning of a reference transaction to extract the components of the transaction that are useful for research. As the data warehouse grows, one line of exploration will be to attempt to automatically classify transactions by type; this will prove useful in creating cleaner search mechanisms and automating reference processes. The NetRef threading issues are a harbinger of the problems to come in attempting to incorporate chat reference into this type of knowledge structure.

Subject-List Interoperability

One of the current challenges in crossing the boundaries between digital reference services, as well as other knowledge-management systems, is that of subject assignments. Most services assign a subject term to a question at some point in the process: the user may assign a subject when the question is asked, the administrator may select a subject explicitly through a field or implicitly through expert assignment, or the expert may assign a topic during the answering process. Many times, these subjects come from a list that is unique to that service.

It is important to maintain the original selection and subject list established by the reference service to aid that service in management and reporting and to help that service work with similar services. From a knowledge-base perspective, however, it is important to map these varying subject lists to a common list to aid in interoperability. Zeng and Chan (2004) presented several approaches to this problem, one of which is switching, in which all individual subject lists are mapped to an intermediary subject list. This is similar to direct mapping except that everything is mapped to one list instead of trying to map all lists to each other. This is currently the approach used by several large multidisciplinary knowledge-base projects, such as HILT ([High-Level Thesaurus Project] Nicholson, Shiri, and McCulloch, 2004) and National Library of Medicine's Metathesaurus (2004).

We are investigating the feasibility of using the HILT thesaurus as the DREW master subject list. To implement it, individual services would work with DREW to develop an appropriate mapping to the HILT subject list. In addition, the original subject terms would be captured in the data warehouse. As the project grows, it may be necessary to create secondary, more specific, metathesauri to allow the mapping between different services focusing on the same topic area.

Privacy

One of the constant concerns about library data is that of patron privacy. The library has traditionally been a safe place for users to gather information. Legislation such as the USA Patriot Act threatens the privacy of patron histories in that it gives government bodies the right to access patron records without the patrons' knowing they are being watched through a roving wiretap

(American Library Association, 2004). In response to this, some libraries are actively deleting and shredding records (Nicholson, 2003). As digital reference services typically collect an e-mail address for a patron, it is possible that they also can be targets for a roving wiretap. If the archives of the service contain personally identifiable information about a patron, then the service would be required to turn over transactions if requested by the appropriate authorities.

In this case, the archival schema for DREW provides a method of protecting the personally identifiable information about a patron while still maintaining the useful information included in the transaction. In addition, the information needed to make administrative decisions is kept. Therefore, the data warehouse balances the need to protect the patron and the need to maintain a data-based history of the service's activities.

There are currently no automated solutions to strip out the personally identifiable information from the content of a reference transaction. This is similar to the problems of de-identification of medical records (Workgroup for Electronic Data Interchange, 2003) which involves removing personal information while the useful information from the records is maintained. An active research area in natural-language processing is the automated identification and replacement of this personal information in medical records. As this research agenda is advanced and solutions are created, we will adapt these medical informatics tools to reference transactions.

THE USEFULNESS OF DREW

This warehouse of digital reference transactions will allow a level of understanding about library services previously unavailable to researchers and educators. In addition, administrators of participating services will gain access to customized reporting and management-information tools as they are developed.

Support of Current Research

There are a number of lines of human intermediation research that would be advanced through the availability of DREW records. One of the challenges for digital reference researchers is getting access to large amounts of cleaned data; DREW will provide a robust source of transactions for these researchers. Those seeking to understand information-seeking behavior or how experts use resources to answer questions would be able to rapidly improve the generalizability of their models through access to data on this scale.

Another line of research that would benefit from this data warehouse is the measurement and evaluation of digital library services. Tools such as bibliomining, or data mining for libraries, require large amounts of cleaned data (Nicholson, 2003). DREW is an ideal place for bibliomining research, and the results will allow the development of new measurement tools for digital reference services and the discovery of novel and actionable patterns existing in the transactions. One goal of this line of research is to create a management-information system that can be applied to the entire database for research purposes, and that participating libraries can access to learn more about their own services.

Informing Service Management and Decision Making

One of the challenges facing individual services is the need for informed management decisions. This call is embodied in evidence-based librarianship, which implores librarians to use the best available evidence when making decisions for their libraries. In addition, librarians are asked to justify their services on a regular basis; many are too busy running their services to step back and create the tools they need to analyze their services appropriately.

As researchers develop methods of measurement and evaluating digital reference services, these tools and models can be integrated into DREW. As these tools are created, managers of individual services can request any of the reports created for the entire warehouse to be run on just the data from their own system. This creates a significant reason for services to participate in the DREW project, as they will then have access to a strong management information system associated with DREW.

Digital reference consortia will also benefit from this relationship, as they can get the same reports and information about their entire consortia. This type of information was previously challenging to discover, but it is essential to strong decision making. As consortia make decisions that can have long-range impact and may not be able to change those decisions easily, it is important that these decisions be powered by the best evidence available.

Modeling the Complex Digital Reference Landscape

One area of research stemming from the use of complexity theory is modeling the digital reference transactions within DREW as a *complex adaptive system*. Once the digital reference transactions have been cleaned, an inductive system of clustering can be used to examine the self-organizing nature of digital reference knowledge bases. Each transaction will be modeled as an autonomous agent with a set of attributes (the proposed DREW element set). Some of the attributes are static (such as the text of the transaction), but some are dynamic (such as the time since the transaction was closed, or the number of times the agent is referred to by other transactions). By placing these transactions in an n-dimensional space (2 or 3 dimensions for visualizing the space, for example), pair-wise comparisons between the agents can be conducted (in essence determining how similar any two agents are). Agents will move "closer" or "farther" apart based upon these comparisons. It is anticipated that these agents will inductively cluster. It is also hypothesized that these clusters will change over time as not only do the dynamic attributes change (a transaction's age, for example), but the agents themselves change (with new questions or new references are added).

CREATING A INFRASTRUCTURE FOR VIRTUAL COLLABORATION

One of the exciting possibilities of a DREW schema is that it empowers the infrastructure to allow for virtual collaboration between researchers and practitioners. Services will start by providing records for DREW. Researchers will then use these records to develop tools across different services. These researchers will then be encouraged to prepare their models and tools using the

DREW schema so that the services participating in DREW can apply these research results to their own services. Practitioners can immediately benefit from research and will be encouraged not only to continue their involvement in DREW but also to improve their management of the digital reference service. Researchers can then test the difference these new tools and models make on reference service, and the cycle continues.

This model is currently in use in the open-source community. As infrastructure and data schema are created, programmers use these to develop tools. As tools are created and released, other programmers improve on the code, and the result is that the users have a much better experience. This virtual collaboration will allow digital reference to rapidly improve as a service.

CONCLUSION: THE DREW RESEARCH AGENDA

The process of creating this digital reference archive introduces a set of questions that power a research agenda. Each of these questions stem from a challenge (a.k.a. opportunity) in the process of creating, implementing, and using this warehouse of digital reference transactions. The development of a common infrastructure would allow collaboration between researchers and services increasing the speed at which we can improve digital reference.

By capturing the artifacts of the human intermediation process through reference authoring, libraries have the ability to produce large amounts of high-quality information. In order to understand this information and create tools that allow for the rapid creation of knowledge bases as well as advance our conceptual understanding of the changing face of reference, researchers need a cleaned collection of transactions from a wide variety of services. The DREW project will supply researchers with this data source and make it possible for participating services to quickly benefit from the results of the research.

REFERENCES

American Library Association. 2004. "The USA Patriot Act and Libraries, 2004" (June), www.ala.org/ala/washoff/WOissues/civilliberties/theusapa-triotact/ usapatriotact.htm (accessed October 18, 2005).

Holland, J. H. 1995. *Hidden Order: How Adaptation Builds Complexity*. New York: Addison Wesley.

Lankes, R. David. 1998. "Building and Maintaining Internet Information Services: K-12 Digital Reference Services." Syracuse, NY: ERIC Clearinghouse on Information & Technology.

Library of Congress. 2004. "NetRef: NISO Committee AZ: Networked Reference Services" (May), www.loc.gov/standards/netref/

National Library of Medicine. 2004. *UMLS Metathesaurus* (June), www.nlm. nih.gov/pubs/factsheets/umlsmeta.htm (accessed October 25, 2005).

Nicholson, Scott. 2003. "Avoiding the Great Data-Wipe of Ought-Three." *American Libraries* 34, no. 9: 36.

Nicholson, Dennis, Ali Shiri, and Emma McCulloch. 2004. "HILT: High-Level Thesaurus Project Phase II" (June), hilt.cdlr.strath.ac.uk/hilt2web/ final-report/0HILT2FinalReport.doc (accessed September 14, 2005).

OCLC. 2004. *Knowledge Base* (July), www.oclc.org/questionpoint/libraries/ knowledge/default.htm (accessed September 14, 2005).

Waldrop, M. M. 1992. *Complexity: The Emerging Science at the Edge of Order and Chaos*. New York: Touchstone.

Workgroup for Electronic Data Interchange. 2004. "De-Identification and Limited Data Set White Paper" (June), www.hipaadvisory.com/action/ WEDIpapers/Deid.pdf (accessed September 15, 2005).

Zeng, M., and L. Chan 2004. *Journal of the American Society for Information Science and Technology* 55, no. 5: 377–395.

PART IV

Creating a Reference Future:
Innovative Approaches

Chapter 7

Managing a Full-Scale, 24/7, Reference Service Consortium: Integrating Specialists from Public and Academic Libraries

Vera Daugaard, Morten Fogh, and Ellen Nielsen

OVERVIEW

This chapter discusses elements that are important in establishing and operating a collaborative public/academic library electronic reference service. It does so within the context of Biblioteksvagten, an electronic reference service operating collaboratively across types of libraries since 2002 to provide electronic reference to Danish citizens. Following the Introduction, which presents a brief history of Biblioteksvagten, the chapter addresses these questions:

- Which elements are important to successfully establish a joint service across library sectors (e.g., the organization, the creation of a shared vision, the formulation of goals and plans, the creation of a Web site, the agreements on cooperation, the formulation of a common working basis)?
- Is it important to create a shared ownership and, if so, how is this obtained?

- How is the necessary information spread out to the different partners?
- What must be done to ensure quality?
- Which elements are important for managing Biblioteksvagten and which qualities must be required of the project manager?
- Is it a good idea to create a national reference service consortium?
- What must be done to guarantee the development of the service?
- How has Biblioteksvagten been marketed?
- What are the plans for the immediate future of Biblioteksvagten?

INTRODUCTION

With financial support from the Danish National Library Authority, Biblioteksvagten was established in 1999 as a pilot project to test the feasibility of a collaborative e-mail/web-based/chat reference service offered to the Danish population in general. After a tentative start, with only 3 participating public libraries and 10 librarians covering the service, by August 2002 Biblioteksvagten had grown to 34 Danish public libraries and just over 150 librarians. Since September 2001 it has been a permanent part of the Danish library service.

Danish academic libraries wanted to offer a similar service and decided to work together on this task across the two sectors. The public libraries' interest in a cooperative venture with the academic libraries was based on the desire to give Biblioteksvagten a greater professional impact by providing the general public and the amateur researcher with easier access to the knowledge and resources of the academic libraries.

The advantages of cooperating led to a joint project between the public libraries and four academic libraries, which in August 2002 was launched as a pilot project with a view to developing a model for future cooperation. Denmark's Electronic Research Library (DEF) provided funding for the pilot project, which ran until the end of the year 2002.

These experiences were so positive that the partnership was consequently made permanent, and further funds were received from DEF for the purpose of buying new, more advanced software to handle all types of inquiries, co-browsing, and more questions. The number of participating libraries has gradually increased, so that in November 2004, the cooperative reference service Biblioteksvagten was staffed with more than 250 librarians from 52 different libraries for 84 manned hours per week:

Monday–Thursday: 8 a.m.–10 p.m.

Friday: 8 a.m.–8 p.m.

Saturday: 8 a.m.–4 p.m.

Sunday: 2 p.m.–10 p.m.

The academic libraries participate Monday–Friday: 8 a.m.–4 p.m.

Figure 7-1 shows a screen-shot of the service.

Figure 7-1
Screen Shot of Biblioteksvagten Service

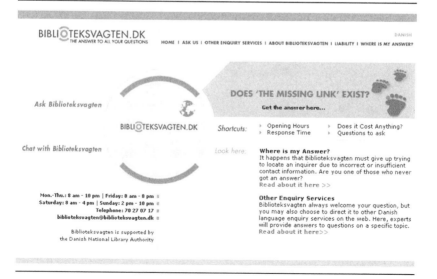

WHICH ELEMENTS ARE IMPORTANT FOR THE SUCCESSFUL ESTABLISHMENT OF A JOINT SERVICE ACROSS LIBRARY SECTORS?

We have found that several elements are important for the success of our joint service, to wit, the organization, the creation of a shared vision, the formulation of goals and plans, the creation of a Web site, the agreements on cooperation, and the formulation of a common working basis. We will focus on them one by one and explain the work involved.

The Organization of Biblioteksvagten

The organization consists of the Steering Committee, two project managers, the Project Team, and the yearly management meeting of the directors of the participating libraries. An important element is the joint Steering Committee, made up of four management representatives from the public libraries, two management representatives from the academic libraries, and the two project managers. The management representatives are elected by managers of the participating libraries at the annual management meeting.

The main tasks of the steering group are

- to work for a continued dynamic development of www. biblioteksvagten.dk as a central service developed by and run by Danish libraries.
- to secure the safeguard of interested parties and the influence of all participating libraries through dialog and interaction.
- to work for an increased use of the service by focusing on quality and customer satisfaction, including systematic quality assessments and measuring customer satisfaction.
- to work for the best possible marketing of www.biblioteksvagten.dk.
- to continue and to develop the project with the library portals www.bibliotek.dk and www.deff.dk.

The Steering Committee sets the general guidelines, while the specific work is done by the Project Team, which includes the two project managers. The Project Team consists of three librarians from the public libraries and three librarians from the academic libraries as well as the two project managers. The steering group appoints the members of the Project Team after receiving recommendations from the participating libraries. No decision has been made yet as to how long the Project Team will continue to serve, but generally speaking, work is being done to adjust the organization of Biblioteksvagten. We will return to the issue later on when dealing with our plans for the near future.

The project managers' closest partners in implementing the tasks assigned by the steering group are the members of the project group. However, the project group also takes initiatives in the development of Biblioteksvagten. The project group is also an important element for a better understanding of the differences between public and academic libraries in order to cooperate in the best possible way.

Once a year, the Steering Committee meets with management representatives from all participating libraries. At this meeting fundamental questions, essential change of politics, and so on, are discussed. If the Steering Committee finds the need for essential changes during the year and the decision cannot wait for the annual meeting, a hearing of the participating libraries is held before any changes are carried through. Depending on the specific situation, an extraordinary management meeting can be called instead. This may happen, for instance, if the financial situation changes considerably.

The organization (steering group, project managers, project group, yearly management meeting) gives the necessary platform for the deliberate work with the other elements listed above (shared vision, goals and plans, Web site, agreements on cooperation, common working basis), and jointly this work has the effect that Biblioteksvagten today is one concerned cross-national inquiry service.

The Vision of Biblioteksvagten

Biblioteksvagten has existed since 1999 with the vision that Danish libraries should play an important role in the citizens' information retrieval and that the service should be present on the Internet. At that time, the development of competence at the participating libraries and among the librarians was included in the plan, and this has today resulted in a distinctly formulated vision for Biblioteksvagten.

The vision is divided into parts, with one aimed at our users:

- The site www.biblioteksvagten.dk is the place to ask questions about everything under the sun.
- Biblioteksvagten helps the user by being visible and accessible when the user needs help from a librarian on the Net.
- Biblioteksvagten offers high-quality, efficient answers to questions.
- The site www.biblioteksvagten.dk is accessible day and night (24/7).

Implicit in these formulations is the Steering Committee's idea that Biblioteksvagten, apart from its own Web site, also wants to cooperate with other Net services as a point of inquiry. The second part of the vision is aimed at the participating libraries: Biblioteksvagten is the central resource for access to the digital information offered by the libraries, and Biblioteksvagten combines the total competence of information retrieval available at the libraries.

This vision led to clear goals established by the Steering Committee:

- that the participating libraries give the work in Biblioteksvagten a very high priority.
- that Biblioteksvagten "plays a lead" in providing access to digital information equal to the role of the individual libraries and, in the long term, perhaps a more important role.
- that a development of competence takes place for each individual librarian who participates.

The Goals and Plan of Action

The vision is not static, however, it may prove to be valid for some years to come. On the basis of the vision, goals for the coming year are developed and a plan of action is made. The goals and plan of action have a clear influence on the government funds that Biblioteksvagten will have at its disposal for the coming year.

At Steering Committee meetings, drafting goals formulations and a plan of action are discussed, and the discussions result in a proposal presented at the annual management meeting. Traditionally, the debate that takes place at the management meetings is lively and engaged, and often the result is that there is a change in the formulation of the goals or adjustments in the plan of action at the following Steering Committee meetings.

Goals and plan of action are explicit and, among other things, there is a clear assignment of responsibility: the Steering Committee, the Project Team, or the project managers. At the annual management meetings, the work done during the past year is evaluated, new goals are set up, and the process begins again.

This "internal" work with goals and a plan of action is carried out parallel with dialog with the state authorities about goals and plan of action. The result of the discussions in this forum has a clear influence on the government funds allotted to Biblioteksvagten in the year to follow.

The Biblioteksvagten Web Site

The Web site of Biblioteksvagten is considered the public image of the initiative, and the external user interface has been changed four times since the inception of the service. We want it to be very easy for Danish citizens to have their questions answered on the Internet. The citizens do not have to speculate whether the question is best answered by a public or academic librarian; they just ask the question at the joint Web site of Biblioteksvagten.

In the early days of the consortium, a specific inquiry form was worked out for the academic libraries, since the public and the academic libraries had very different types of information that the inquirer *must* give when asking the question. The experiences gained from the first year have resulted in the development of a joint inquiry form.

The librarians from the two sectors each work from their respective administrative Web sites. However, all have access to both Web sites, so it is very easy to pass on questions to one another should a question end up in the wrong place.

The Agreements of Cooperation

The cooperation between the many libraries and between the two sectors has been defined in an overall description of the organization, as mentioned earlier, but no specific contract between the parties has been drawn up. Biblioteksvagten is very much based on a common interest in making it succeed—and as mentioned earlier, we will deal with our plans for a future organizational change later on.

The concept of "Agreements of Cooperation" stipulates the degree of involvement of the individual library in Biblioteksvagten. This includes the resources invested in the work, how the work can be done, and so on. In addition, these agreements provide guidance about the practical cooperation between the individual libraries and between the two library sectors. The "Agreements of Cooperation" is found in the description of the organization as well as in the manuals on the two administrative Web sites.

Even in a small country like Denmark, library size varies in both public and academic libraries. Since the vision of Biblioteksvagten includes development of competence for Danish librarians, it makes sense to offer small libraries the opportunity to participate with a "shared place." Two small public libraries occupy one place in Biblioteksvagten. Within the field of academic libraries, the difference in size is taken into consideration when arranging timetables.

So far the academic libraries contribute 40 staff hours per week. Therefore, it has been agreed that the public libraries watch both administrative Web sites during evening and weekend hours, answer the questions when it can be justified professionally, and at least give first aid.

The organization chart confers the overall project management on the project manager for the public libraries. This is important in the preparation of the Steering Committee meeting, among other things. However, in practice, the two project managers work together very closely, which contributes to maintain Biblioteksvagten as one joint service.

Common Working Guidelines

The last element to address is the set of Biblioteksvagten's common service guidelines. These guidelines consist of nine statements that are the result of a dialog between the librarians involved, and together these statements form "the framework" for the answers Biblioteksvagten gives and, thus, the framework for Biblioteksvagten's "product."

The nine statements are as follows:

1. The inquirer should have a concrete answer or be helped a step further.
2. Quality instead of quantity.
3. The answer is to be adjusted to the needs of the inquirer.
4. The answer is to be given in a friendly and positive tone.
5. The aim should be to refer to Web resources when giving an answer.
6. The answer should contain the sources used.
7. Whenever possible, an answer should be given within 24 hours.
8. It is recommended that the librarian end with "Please do ask again if the answer is not satisfactory."
9. "The desk" should be cleared, if possible, at the end of the day.

These guidelines have not been finalized. They are discussed continuously, and adjustments are made, since it is important that all librarians bear these statements in mind when they work in our joint service. The nine statements are an internal set of guidelines. A specific service declaration has been made for the users so that they know what to expect from Biblioteksvagten.

IS IT IMPORTANT TO CREATE A SHARED OWNERSHIP, AND, IF SO, HOW IS THIS OBTAINED?

The creation of one joint service across the two sectors is only possible and actually only of any interest if it is possible to

succeed in creating and maintaining a shared ownership of the
service on the part of each individual librarian working in Biblioteksvagten. Therefore, precisely this ownership has been on
the agenda at every seminar held in Biblioteksvagten since its
tender start in 1999.

It is beneficial for Biblioteksvagten that there is a project
manager from both the public and the academic libraries because of the differences in culture in the two library sectors. At
the same time, it is also of importance that the two project
managers work closely together, and that they know each
other's sector. In this way, we avoid attitudes like "those people
from the other sector." The project managers are known in both
sectors, so there is a feeling that they both stand for the same
thing.

One or more seminars/workshops are held yearly. Here
the discussions are about model types/collection of examples
and other procedures from the manual. At these seminars, li-
brary/reference subjects are presented by people from outside
Biblioteksvagten, and time is spent on training of new librarians
in Biblioteksvagten, instruction in new software, and so on.

A continuous dialog between the Steering Committee, the
Project Team, the project managers, and the participating libraries is facilitated by the appointment of a contact from each
library. The contacts are in charge locally of the work in Biblioteksvagten and they are kept informed about the various initiatives to develop the service so that they are able to give input
and thus influence the work.

HOW IS THE NECESSARY INFORMATION
DISSEMINATED TO THE DIFFERENT PARTNERS?

The steering group and the project managers agree that by far
the most important element to achieve and maintain ownership
of Biblioteksvagten is the possibility of having contributory influence on the service, and this influence can only be exerted if
you get the necessary information. Therefore, communication
guidelines for Biblioteksvagten have been established. The contents of these guidelines can briefly be summarized as follows:
The guidelines are a description of which information is sent to

whom, when, how, and in which form. In addition, communication guidelines also describe the communication with the users.

A common mailing list is used to send mass messages from the project managers, but it also makes it possible for an individual librarian to ask for help or to send a problem to the network and thus influence the development of Biblioteksvagten.

The cooperation in Biblioteksvagten is mostly practiced as "distance cooperation," and, therefore, to a large extent the cooperation is based on written communication between the parties—via the Net/e-mail. Of course, the librarians working in Biblioteksvagten also use the phone, but written communication is by far the most prevalent, and both the organization and these communication conventions have been built to enhance cooperation. The development of a manual for each administrative homepage has been useful in order to maintain the great amount of information exchanged, to maintain agreements on the cooperation, and, not least, to describe all the small but nevertheless important working procedures.

Another important part of the information exchange is the minutes from the different meetings and seminars. The minutes are sent to the relevant persons, but they are also posted to the administrative Web site so that all librarians working in Biblioteksvagten have an opportunity to follow the development as reflected through meetings and seminars.

WHAT MUST BE DONE TO ENSURE QUALITY?

The continued existence of Biblioteksvagten—as a joint national inquiry service with a well-developed feeling of ownership shared by all the participating librarians—is dependent on the high quality of the answers we supply. Therefore, improving the quality of the answers has been on the agenda as long Biblioteksvagten has existed.

The formulation of the nine statements in the common working guidelines was the first step in the work to secure the quality. Soon after, minimum requirements to giving answers to a series of types of questions were formulated—and today an actual collection of examples has been compiled. This is not to be considered a key, but a help, to the individual librarian: Will this answer be sufficient? Should I go further? Do I give too many references?

The collection of examples, the minimum requirements, and so forth, are found in the manual, together with detailed descriptions of how to actually work with the questions. The individual librarian will thus always be able to find out about the requirements of each level of answer in Biblioteksvagten.

The way to give feedback on the work of the individual librarian in Biblioteksvagten differs in the public and the academic libraries, since the academic libraries generally are dealing with specific subject areas while the public libraries are looking at general subjects of all kinds. The librarians from the public libraries get feedback from a so-called feedback group, that is, a group consisting of participating librarians from seven public libraries.

The intention of the feedback group is to see to it that the individual librarian becomes "smarter" (more clever), and that, at the same time, Biblioteksvagten helps the inquirers to get good answers. It is important that the answers given to the users are formulated in a clear and exact way. An agreement has been made about how both positive and negative feedback is to be given. This has been sent to all participating librarians, and it has been agreed that the work in the feedback group is to be done in turns, hoping that the work is considered a constructive feedback and not a supervision or criticism.

As far as the establishment of the feedback group, a course was held on how to give feedback, and this course proved to be so rewarding that it was agreed that all participating librarians should have a corresponding mini-course.

Quality assurance in the academic libraries is carried out at the library that has answered the question. This model was chosen precisely because the academic libraries differ very much in subject areas. For example, it is difficult for an agriculture library to assess the quality of the answers given from a technical library. The project manager checks that the formal requirements to the answers are OK, that is, the filling in of the answer form, and that the minimum requirements to the answers are observed.

Generally, the participating librarians are qualified librarians or they have another relevant education. Principally, the work in Biblioteksvagten is not different from the work at the local library. However, in connection with entering the consortium the individual librarian will, of course, be fully prepared for the work, partly through training in the specific working procedures, but, what is equally important, he or she will be introduced to the common working guidelines, the minimum requirements, and a sense of ownership of Biblioteksvagten. This work is continued by running project days. The work on these occasions is often focused on quality issues, with discussion papers from both external introductory speakers and from the project managers. Also, discussions are an important element on these days, since the project managers have thoughts and expectations about the work in the participating libraries being harmonious. Here the librarians are able to talk with one another, and often these talks result in changes and additions to the manual.

FACTORS TO CONSIDER

Managing Biblioteksvagten is both exciting job and demanding due to several factors.

Only Virtual Contact in the Day-to-Day Work

The majority of communication between the project manager and the individual librarian is virtual. There is an advantage to those who have had the possibility of getting to know each other before, since it is always easier to communicate with a person you know.

Many Corporate Cultures

The two library sectors have very different cultures when it comes to how much service the librarians give their users. It is traditional in public libraries to try to find the answer, not only to help to find out how you find the answer. One of the primary user groups of the academic libraries are students—it applies

to the direct inquiries as well as the inquiries received via Biblioteksvagten, and here the information retrieval forms part of
the education. Therefore, suggestions and guidance on how to
find the needed information in relevant databases most often is
the service that is given in the academic libraries.

In the virtual service of the users, answers are given to questions about specific facts, usually with references to a few books
and articles about the subjects in question. Likewise, references
are often given to Web addresses where it is possible to find further information.

Geographical and Dimensional Dispersion

While Denmark is a small country, the culture differs quite a bit
from place to bridge. For example, the Copenhagen libraries are
quite different from the larger libraries of the provinces. In addition, the cultures in large and a small library differ. This does
not mean that the poorest service is in small libraries; on the
contrary, in small libraries the users are well known, and, therefore, it is easier to find the correct answer for them. The same
thing applies to academic libraries. A small library in such cases
often is closely related to a middle-range educational institution, where staff have quite detailed knowledge of the syllabi
and courses.

Lack of Formal Competence

The project managers are not formally in charge of the librarians working in Biblioteksvagten, and the fact that a library is
participating in Biblioteksvagten does not always mean that a
high priority is given at the management level of the library.
Here it is important to reach the managers at the annual management meeting. The project managers' dilemma is that the interests of the library outweigh those of Biblioteksvagten, and
the project managers have no management authority over the
individual librarians. The project manager is the manager of
people who have another manager as well, someone they report
to during the major part of their working hours! It is important
that the participating libraries share the fundamental opinion

that the whole library (that is, all the staff members) participates in Biblioteksvagten. In this way, all the staff members are
contributing to the marketing of Biblioteksvagten, and also they
get to appreciate that the need for extra assistance may arise
among their colleagues.

Qualifications of a Good Project Manager

Besides general professional managerial qualifications, the
project manager of Biblioteksvagten needs to have several
characteristics.

Ability to Establish Good Personal Relationships

Seminars, courses, and meetings are among the opportunities
that particularly serve this purpose, where it is important to include the social element. The ground for a good cooperation is
respect towards one another—and this respect is created by getting to know one another's strengths. It is exceptionally important when you work "in virtual space" that you feel confident
with one another, and the key word here is acquaintance with
one another.

Ability to Create and Develop Positive Team Spirit

It is important that everyone involved pull together. In Biblioteksvagten everyone's work contributes to create a common
identity as one inquiry service.

Ability to Inspire and Motivate

Since no formal training is given, this ability to inspire and mo-
tivate is absolutely crucial in Biblioteksvagten. If there are many
questions that remain to be answered, it is vital that the staff
can be increased quickly—and this means that the individual
librarian should feel inclined to contribute even though he or
she perhaps is not to be on duty that day.

Ability to Formulate One's Thoughts in Writing

Since the day-to-day management is mainly carried out in writing (e-mails), it is extremely important that the messages are

formulated with care. It is an art to express oneself clearly and precisely so that there is no misunderstanding.

THE VALIDITY OF THE IDEA

Is it a good idea for more than 200 librarians from more than 50 libraries to cooperate on one joint service? Since Denmark is small—there are only five million inhabitants in the whole country—cooperation is necessary. Joint access to the materials of all the Danish libraries has been achieved with the creation of the database www.bibliotek.dk. Biblioteksvagten, in its capacity as the "Net librarian," is thus a fine supplement to this database. Our service has a good chance of making its way through the information jungle to the citizens if the citizens only have to remember one Web address instead of a series of different addresses (such as local, regional, subject specific).

The fact that more than 200 librarians cooperate in one joint service and, thus, have the opportunity to learn from one another spurs professional growth that is of local benefit to the users of an individual library. For instance, a librarian who works at a small provincial library is not challenged professionally to the same extent as a librarian who works in a large town with many university students. Participation in Biblioteksvagten makes up for this drawback. Eventually, the increased qualification of the Danish corps of librarians will be of benefit to the Danish library system in general. It is possible for the network to become too large. It is important that individual librarians keep in touch with the work through activities, such as by regularly answering questions. Otherwise, the feeling of ownership may be lost, with the consequence of decreasing quality.

The possibility of splitting up the service into a series of regional inquiry services might be considered; however, the Steering Committee has more confidence in the possibility of rotating the participating libraries. For instance, if you have participated for a period of five years, you get the chance to withdraw, and another library takes over the job. This arrangement would also solve the problem of primary users in some libraries making use of the service of Biblioteksvagten without any contribution from the local library.

WHAT MUST BE DONE TO SECURE THE DEVELOPMENT OF THE SERVICE?

The very determined work with goal formulations and preparation of plans of action, done by the Steering Committee and the Project Team, makes sure, in the short run, at least, that Biblioteksvagten does not stagnate. Also the involvement of all the participating librarians via the mailing list results in good input.

In addition, the "creation of networks," to which Biblioteksvagten has contributed for a number of years, secures development at several levels.

- *At the National Level*
  In Denmark a large number of Net libraries are members of the Association of Danish Internet-based Public Library Consortia Projects. A network of project managers has been established, partly in order to provide a forum for debate regarding the managerial aspects, however, the network also results in good ideas for developing the service of Biblioteksvagten.
- *At the Scandinavian Level*
  Biblioteksvagten is in good contact with "sister services" in Sweden, Norway, and Finland, and the project managers have actively participated in several Scandinavian seminars, both by presenting discussion papers and as active listeners.
- *At the International Level*
  Biblioteksvagten participated for the second time in the Virtual Reference Desk (VRD) Conference. Biblioteksvagten has also been a contributor in the context of IFLA. Consequently, Biblioteksvagten has gradually managed to establish an almost international network—and indeed the project managers are drinking in all good ideas, especially being in the U.S.

HOW HAS BIBLIOTEKSVAGTEN BEEN MARKETED?

From the very beginning, the Steering Committee was aware of the fact that Biblioteksvagten was considered a competitor by many Danish libraries because it aims its service at all Danish citizens and,thus, answers questions that normally would be answered by the local library. Therefore, the first marketing initiative in 1999 was a letter sent to all Danish public libraries to minimize the competitive aspect. The idea of Biblioteksvagten was explained and the Steering Committee encouraged the libraries to add a link to Biblioteksvagten to their own Web site, and about one-third did so.

Other initiatives were press releases, contacts with local radio stations, and the production of bookmarks, which were placed in libraries and book stores all over the country for three weeks. Articles to library journals were written and a pamphlet and poster were produced and distributed in local libraries.

Biblioteksvagten's status as a permanent service as of September 2001 was supposed to be celebrated with a kick-off event on September 13. Press releases were sent to both local and national newspapers, radio and television stations—and many of them responded. Local television and local radio stations contacted Biblioteksvagten and presented the service in their programs. An agreement with the national broadcasting company, Danmarks Radio, was made, but then "9/11" happened, so events were postponed. Later on, the event took place and some merchandising effects (mouse pads, pamphlets, and banners) were produced and distributed by the participating libraries.

Since then, all Danish libraries have been used as platforms for the marketing of Biblioteksvagten, and new marketing materials (posters, bookmarks, postcards, mobiles, etc.) corresponding with the changing of the Web site have been produced and distributed.

The Web site has, of course, been reported to several search engines, and this autumn experiments will be made with actual advertisements in a series of magazines within the education system. Besides, agreements on cooperation with several Net libraries have been made (among others, the national database www.bibliotek.dk), which means that these Net libraries contribute indirectly to the marketing of Biblioteksvagten.

WHAT ARE THE PLANS FOR THE IMMEDIATE
FUTURE OF BIBLIOTEKSVAGTEN?

There are several items planned for the immediate future.

The Formation of an Association

The cooperation in Biblioteksvagten has not been confirmed by any kind of contract, as already mentioned. The individual manager declares verbally, or in writing, that his library would like to join the consortium, and the library is admitted. The management of Biblioteksvagten can do practically nothing if a library suddenly declares that it no longer has sufficient funds to continue the participation. Cooperation in Biblioteksvagten has become too comprehensive for this very loose "project organization." Therefore, a decision was made at last year's management meeting to work towards the formation of an actual association, and a draft of bylaws will be on the agenda of the management meeting this year.

New Chat Software

In connection with the entry of academic libraries into Biblioteksvagten, it was decided that a new and more advanced chat software should be purchased, and an agreement was made with the firm LSSI/Tutor.com for a test period of Virtual Reference Toolkit and Ref Tracker. Unfortunately, we had to admit at the end of the test period that the software did not correspond with our needs, and it was decided to discontinue the relationship with Tutor.com. Instead, the steering group is considering entering into a contract with the firm Kommuneinformation (Danish representative of the Norwegian firm Sentinel) regarding the chat software eDialog24. So far this software has no satisfactory cobrowsing feature, and that is why other software products (e.g., VRLplus) are still being considered.

Reprogramming of the Administrative Web Site

A negotiation with another firm about reprogramming the whole of the administrative Web site is conducted. This is to

better prepare Biblioteksvagten to act as the inquiry box for
other Net services.

Cooperation

Among the plans for the future of Biblioteksvagten, a high priority is given to extended cooperation with the joint Danish
database www.bibliotek.dk so that Biblioteksvagten very
clearly appears to be "Denmark's Net Librarian."

CONCLUSION

One of the core values of libraries is to supply citizens, compa-
nies, and institutions with correct and reliable information. It is
precisely because of this that libraries have always enjoyed a
special status in society. Even though the libraries are financed
by public funds and owned by the state and local authorities in
Denmark, they do not act as if they were "part of the Establishment," nor are they considered to be so. On the contrary, the libraries are considered to be free institutions, independent of
economic, political, and religious interests.

The Danish librarians are proud of this almost constitutional
sacredness. Therefore, it is also natural that one of the first Internet-based services from the libraries became an inquiry service, that is Biblioteksvagten. Even though the libraries have
gradually developed a wide range of national services on the
Internet, Biblioteksvagten continues to be the flagship that
guarantees free and reliable information for all.

The libraries that are participating in Biblioteksvagten are
characterized as being a little more ambitious, competent, and
visionary than the others. To participate in Biblioteksvagten is a
mark of quality, and there is a waiting list for those who want to
join.

With Biblioteksvagten the successful establishment of a quality inquiry service has taken place, and here all interested parties
within the library field stand together, whether they represent
the state or the local authorities, whether large or small, or
whether they have generous funding or very little. The libraries
in Denmark have a historic tradition for cooperation regarding

common institutions. Biblioteksvagten is a modern common resource that is based on formation of networks, professionalism,
equal status, and respect.

Link to Web Site:
www.biblioteksvagten.dk/(Danish)
www.biblioteksvagten.dk/english/index.asp (English)

REFERENCES
(Only literature written in English is cited.)

Daugaard, Vera. 2000. Net Librarian: A Danish National Online Information
    Service. Paper presented at Virtual Reference Desk VRD Conference—
    The Second Annual Digital Reference Conference, "Facets of Digital Ref-
    erence" (October 16–17), Seattle, Wash., www.vrd.org/conferences/
    VRD2000/proceedings/Daugaard12-14.shtml (accessed September 15,
    2005).
Daugaard, Vera. 2001. "Net Librarian—A Danish "Ask the Librarian-Service."
    Tidskrift för Dokumentation 56, no. 4: 113–120.
Daugaard, Vera. 2003. The Co-operation across Cultures in Public and Scien-
    tific Libraries: The Co-operation in Net Librarian/Biblioteksvagten: A
    Danish "Ask the Librarian" Service. Paper presented at World Library
    and Information Congress: 69th IFLA General Conference and Council
    (August 1–9), Berlin, www.ifla.org/IV/ifla69/papers/106e-Daugaard.pdf
    (accessed September 15, 2005).
Daugaard, Vera, and Susanne Dalsgaard Krag. 2003. "Net Librarian: A joint
    project." *Scandinavian Public Library Quarterly* 36, no. 1, www.splq.info/
    issues/vol36_1/03.htm (accessed October 25, 2005).

Chapter 8

Creating a Knowledge Base: Analyzing a Veteran Reference Librarian's Brain

Charles Early, Andrea Japzon, and Sarah Endres

OVERVIEW

Virtual reference transactions provided a solution to a knowledge-management problem at the NASA Goddard Space Flight Center Library. Online reference services, real-time and e-mail, allow for the development of a knowledge base. One hundred e-mail question-and-answer pairs were analyzed to reveal the steps taken and the sources used by a soon-to-retire librarian. A guide to the information sources and producers at Goddard was created. Given the dynamic nature of information at Goddard, a database built on the Apache, MySQL, PHP (AMP) open source platform was designed for the guide. The resource is now dynamic and can continue to grow with input from all Goddard's librarians.

INTRODUCTION

Goddard Space Flight Center is located in Greenbelt, Maryland, 10 miles northeast of Washington, D.C., and was established by the National Aeronautics and Space Administration (NASA) as its center for space research in 1959, soon after the agency was founded. It has become one of the world's leading research establishments, with the largest scientific staff of any of the NASA field centers. Nearly 6,000 scientists and engineers work at Goddard, in addition to well over a thousand contractors working for Goddard at nearby off-site locations. These people are the Goddard Library's main users.

Goddard's primary mission today is building, designing, and using scientific research satellites in Earth's orbit (along with the scientific instruments and observatories they carry). These include astronomical satellites such as the Hubble Space Telescope and earth observation satellites such as Landsat and the weather satellites that Goddard builds for the National Oceanic and Atmospheric Administration. In support of this primary mission, Goddard also maintains a network of satellites and ground stations for tracking and data communications, and several enormous digital repositories of data from the satellites. These activities all pose major engineering challenges.

Engineering, especially the cutting-edge, highly specialized sort of engineering that goes on at Goddard, relies heavily on unconventional, often fugitive, information resources. For example, these resources include technical reports, standards and specifications, engineering drawings, design guidelines, and lessons learned. Institutional (Goddard and NASA) information and knowledge resources are essential for Goddard engineers, but scattered and difficult to locate.

NASA's Scientific and Technical Information Program was a pioneer in the use of computers to manage information in the early 1960s (see www.sti.nasa.gov). Today it maintains a database of nearly 4 million citations to aerospace-related documents and makes a collection of over 1.2 million technical reports available in hard copy and electronically through the Center for Aerospace Information. Other NASA information systems include the online union catalog of the NASA Center libraries, a database of NASA and other standards and specifications, a database of NASA directives and regulations, a metasearch engine for the many NASA photo and multimedia collections, and still others. Additional information resources are scattered among the thousands of NASA and Goddard Web sites. Some important documents are still available only in hardcopy in undisclosed locations. Bibliographic control is excellent for the major NASA databases, and poor to nonexistent for everything else.

When Goddard begins a new project to design and build a satellite, an ad hoc work group is formed. The design and construction process generates hundreds or thousands of technical documents: plans and drawings, design reviews, modifications, test results, and so forth. These documents need to be managed while they are being used by the project, and a project library is set up. This library is intended only for use by the project group, and usually little or no effort is made to offer any sort of access to anyone else. Once the project is completed and the satellite is launched, these documents are warehoused and forgotten, and much valuable and reusable knowledge is forgotten with them. Some progress has been made in improving this situation. The Goddard engineering librarian, Early, maintains a directory of active project librarians and a mailing list for project librarians who will cooperate and share knowledge. There is a Goddard-wide database, the Centralized Configuration Management System, that holds about 10,000 documents from some Goddard projects, but it is incomplete and limited in scope.

VIRTUAL REFERENCE A SOLUTION TO A KNOWLEDGE-MANAGEMENT PROBLEM

Because some institutional information sources are extremely decentralized, poorly documented, and poorly archived, the Goddard Library has depended almost entirely on the experience and tacit knowledge base of Early, the senior librarian, who is soon to retire, to handle this class of reference requests. There was essentially no backup. A new solution for answering difficult reference questions was needed to provide a means for new or less experienced staff to answer questions without Early. First, the relevant and helpful knowledge possessed by Early needed to be identified. Once identified, it need be captured and made accessible at future points of need. While Goddard presents a particularly complex information environment, most libraries deal with the same problem on some level.

Libraries have always sought to make explicit, that is, to codify or articulate knowledge for the purpose of documentation, the tacit knowledge of reference librarians. "Tacit knowledge is intuitive and practice-based, which makes it both valuable and difficult to pass on to others" (Stover, 2004). Historically, reference departments have employed a hard-copy card file rolodex-style system for capturing and updating difficult to find information. The Ithaca (N.Y.) College Library and Multnomah County (Ore.) Public Libraries provide early examples of libraries employing online technologies to create a knowledge base for reference work. Ithaca populated a File-Maker Pro database with questions from the reference department card file and then expanded the knowledge base from there. Multnomah used e-mail to track and ticket the workflow of reference requests while using a database engine to control and organize question answering (Perez, 1999).

The reference librarians of New Brunswick (N.J.) Campus Libraries of Rutgers University created CKDB, the common knowledge database, as a means of sharing knowledge across campus libraries and to aid librarians in answering unfamiliar discipline-specific questions. (See http://ckdb.rutgers.edu to access the knowledge base.) CKDB is reported to have improved communication across campus libraries; however, the process of contributing to the database is not embedded, but voluntary. Therefore, stories about the steps taken to find answers to difficult reference questions are not routinely or systematically captured in the database (Jantz, 2001). Questions answered at a reference desk rather than via a virtual reference system are more difficult to archive as the process of answering a question is not automatically captured.

The Web-based Ready Reference Database (RRD) at San Diego (Calif.) State University provides a highly structured example of a reference knowledge base. The RRD project leader actively collects information from the reference staff through both formal and informal means. Then, the leader determines which aspects of the information provided are most critical and relevant to the information that already exists in the database. Through this process, the leader maintains the database with updates and cross-references (Stover, 2004). Thus, the RRD provides access to valuable information but not to steps taken to obtain the information.

Online reference services, real-time and e-mail, facilitate the development of knowledge bases. With virtual reference transactions, a tangible artifact is created with each exchange, which is usually stored automatically. Librarians can now archive particularly meaningful exchanges to be used again to answer future questions. With this, the potential exists to record the tacit knowledge of reference librarians making explicit their knowledge, which users and library staff can learn from. The transcripts from real-time sessions and e-mail correspondence provide a new vantage point for studying reference staff behavior, the research process, and resource usage. For example, the Digital Reference Education Initiative (DREI) provides access to both good and bad chat reference transactions for the purpose of teaching the reference interview through real interactions (see http://drei.syr.edu/item_list.cfm?NavJD=22).

OCLC's QuestionPoint is both a service and a product. In addition to being a tool for managing virtual reference exchanges, QuestionPoint is a searchable global knowledge base that is created by, and provided to, all its customers. The acquisition of 24/7, a chat reference service, by OCLC will no doubt expand the 1,000 libraries using the product and thereby increase the over 7,000 question-and-answer pairs in the database (OCLC, 2004). The knowledge base has the potential to save librarians time and to provide knowledge of new resources through the collective sharing of the knowledge and experience of many reference librarians.

The knowledge base is a tool of knowledge management in that it provides a means of generating, capturing, and sharing the knowledge contained within. The value of human and intellectual capitals has increased because of the current state of information economy (Hirsh and Dinkelacker, 2004). Given this, the United States government and the corporate sector have struggled with ways of keeping the knowledge of employees long after retirement (Liebowitz, 2002; Hoffman and Hanes, 2003). They are seeking ways to formalize or codify knowledge, that is shared or used in an informal manner (Liebowitz, 2002).

The knowledge of scientific and technical workers provides the most tangible examples of the problems that can arise when knowledge is not documented. Technology changes at a rapid pace, and infrastructures based on that technology often do not change as rapidly. In the case of NASA, the loss of engineers from the Apollo Era meant a loss of their knowledge (Hoffman and Hanes, 2003). The Electric Power Research Institute (EPRI) study of electric utilities workers found that manuals and procedures were not effective tools for eliciting tacit knowledge leaving much knowledge undocumented (Gross, Hanes, and Ayres, 2002).

As in the examples of library reference knowledge bases detailed above, most library knowledge-management systems/resources capture explicit knowledge: topical resources, location of resources, and the best possible resources for different query types. These systems do not typically succeed at capturing tacit knowledge: knowing how to find information, what is available, how to select relevant sources, and how to follow a path to the right information (Gandhi, 2004). The EPRI study recommends devising a plan to elicit, store, retrieve, and present knowledge when needed. It could be argued that virtual reference systems do just that for the knowledge of reference librarians. While Bill Katz's (2002) two-volume introduction to reference services provides a vital piece of instruction for reference librarians, the transcripts from virtual reference transactions have the potential to document the tacit knowledge of librarians, thereby detailing a fuller understanding.

DEVELOPMENT OF THE GUIDE

Like most reference departments, for years the Goddard Library has kept a log of reference questions. Questions answered in person, over the phone, and via e-mail are transferred to an Excel spreadsheet. In the process, the details of the transaction are greatly reduced. In March of 2004, a chat reference service was launched at the library. The service automatically generates a record of each reference transaction, thereby creating a knowledge base of questions and answers. This service, unlike e-mail reference, is not well used at Goddard. So Early and Japzon began to populate the knowledge base with entries from the

Excel question log in an effort to create a tool for answering questions. They found that this Q&A resource provided little orientation for librarians in this information environment. Where does one begin, and how does one get access to the right question to begin answering the current question? As mentioned previously, a significant amount of information at Goddard is produced from many different internal projects and is not centrally managed. The goal became to organize Early's knowledge and navigation of Goddard and NASA information rather than organizing the sources of information.

Early suggested emulating the Department of Defense's (DOD) *How to Get It Guide* (Doezema and Fox, 1998). This is a print volume updated at irregular intervals that is intended to aid individuals in accessing DOD information. Early and Japzon sat down together with pen and paper waiting for Early's knowledge about Goddard to surface in an orderly manner. This was not a productive effort. They found they needed some cues to elicit the knowledge from Early. They went back to Questions & Answers for the cues. Early randomly selected 100 previously asked questions from the outbox of his e-mail account. They tried again, this time with Endres, the cataloger/reference librarian, and began to describe and classify the information sources and the information producers at Goddard that were used to answer the questions.

After the review of approximately 70 questions, the point of diminishing returns was reached. It took much longer to analyze the first questions than later ones. The mention of a resource or an agency produced a mental association with others in Early's mind, and these resources were documented along with the steps he took to answer the questions. The result was 160 distinct entries for either information resources or producers related to Goddard.

The entries were added to an HTML document and were organized into four categories: NASA documents, technical reports, open literature, and images and multimedia. As the list of resources increased, it became more difficult to keep the HTML document organized and properly formatted. It was then decided to transfer the information to an AMP platform database, which was created by one of the library staff.[1]

Various decisions were made regarding the format of each record and the standards for entering information. We decided to separate the entry into several parts: title, URL, description, and keywords. The title and URL have a specific format to which they should adhere, and a style sheet was created to help people enter their information in the correct format. After discussing the benefits of a controlled vocabulary versus uncontrolled keywords, the team decided that uncontrolled keywords would be of greater use. The person entering the information in the database could type in any keyword he or she thinks a user might enter to find this information. Figure 8-1 illustrates the search results for the keyword search *standards*.

Once the database structure was created, it was necessary to decide who would be using the database and who would be updating it. Since the guide would have resources that are limited to Goddard employees, either because of license agreements or security restrictions, it was decided to keep the guide limited to users within the Goddard domain. However, the perceived primary users of the guide, and the only ones adding to

Figure 8-1
Search Results for the Keyword *Standards*

Office of Scientific and Technical Information (OSTI)	http://www.osti.gov/	Office of Scientific and Technical Information of the U.S. Departr Energy (DOE). The information clearinghouse for DOE and its predecessor agencies ERDA (Energy Research and Developme Administration, 1974-1977) and AEC...more
Office of System Safety and Mission Assurance Office of System Safety and Mission Assurance (OSSMA)	n/a	A major division of GSFC (Code 300). Formerly OFA. See Code Specifications. more
Orbital Information Group	http://oig1.gsfc.nasa.gov	A group within the Space Communications Program which mair database of detailed information about the orbits of all artificial s in Earth orbit. The database also has information about man-ma debris i...more
Outgassing Handbook	http://outgassing.nasa.gov/	A searchable database information about gasses given off by va materials under vacuum conditions, derived from tests conducte GSFC from 1967 through the present. Available in print form as Outgassing Data for Selecting Spacecraft Materials ...more
Parts Information	n/a	Engineers often need to know technical specifications for parts considering using in a design (electronic components in particul Mechanical Engineering Library has a sitewide licence for acce: collection of vendor catalogs at h...more
Procurement-related Information	n/a	The NASA Aquisition Internet Service (http://nais.nasa.gov/) ha: extensive information resources for anyone involved in doing bus with NASA, including the NASA Procurement Reference Library includes the NASA Procurement Management System (...more

the database, are the library staff and the various project librarians located in different buildings on campus. To maintain quality control of the database, any entry created goes into a temporary database, where it is then reviewed by one of the reference librarians before being added into the permanent database. This allows the records to be edited for corrections. Figure 8-2 shows an example of a database entry.

Now that the database has been created, and the entries added, how does one find the correct entry? Three different ways of finding the correct entry were devised: searching, internal linking, and a show-all feature. The searching feature currently searches every field in the record. There are four kinds of searches to choose from: *substring* (which is the default), *AND*, *OR*, and *exact phrase*. For most purposes, the sub-string search is the most useful as it searches for any record that contains the string of characters somewhere in the text, even if the string is

Figure 8-2
Example of a Database Entry

NASA Handbook (NHB)

URL: *n/a*

NASA Handbook, a series of NASA directives that have been superseded first by NPG, NASA Procedures and Guidelines, and since December 12, 2003 by NPR, NASA Procedural Requirements. Likewise, the GHB (Goddard Handbook) series has become GPG, and similarly for other NASA centers. The series NMI (NASA Management Instruction) is now NPG (NASA Policy Guideline); similarly for GSFC and the other centers. The Cancelled Directives Report from NODIS has the history and current replacements (if any) of NHBs and NMIs, as well as more recent directives.

- NASA Handbook 5300.4 (NHB5300.4)
  A group of 15 directives related to quality assurance and workmanship. All parts of NHB5300.4 were cancelled around 1996. Some were first converted into NASA Assurance Standards (NAS) with the corresponding number for a brief period. (See http://www.hq.nasa.gov/office/codeq/doctree/docgenis.htm). Their replacements, if any, are listed below:
    o NHB 5300.4 (1A - 1): Deleted. Partially replaced by NASA STD 8729.1 and NSTS 5300.4 (1D - 2), Chapter 3.
    o NHB 5300.4 (1B): Replaced by NPD 8730.3 (superseded by NPD 1280.1) and the industry standard ANSI/ISO/ASQC-Q9001-2000 (an ISO 9000 standard).
    o NHB 5300.4 (1C): Replaced by NPD 8730.3 (superseded by NPD 1280.1) and the industry standard ANSI/ISO/ASQC-Q9002-1994 (an ISO 9000 standard).
    o NHB 5300.4 (1D - 2): Replaced by NSTS 5300.4 (1D - 2).
    o NHB 5300.4 (1E): Deleted.
    o NHB 5300.4 (1F): Deleted.
    o NHB 5300.4 (1G): Deleted.
    o NHB 5300.4 (2B - 3): Replaced by NPG 8735.2 (now NPR 8735.2).

within a longer word. Internal linking was also added, so if a user found mention in a record of a hyperlinked resource of interest, a click on the word links to the entry about that resource. The last method of record retrieval is just to comb through all the records using the *show all* feature.

IMPLEMENTING THE DATABASE

The entries from the HTML guide were copied into the database and keywords added to each record. Then, two of the reference librarians did a quality-control check of the database: editing records, removing duplicate entries, merging other records together, and adding internal linking (which did not transfer from the HTML document). The librarians then tested the database for ease of use and came up with a few corrections, which were then implemented. A cheat sheet was created to help users search the database and enter new records. A training session was held for the library staff and project librarians in which the different features were demonstrated and any questions answered. The database is not a finished product, so users are encouraged to provide feedback via e-mail, phone, or an online survey.

Plans are progressing to enhance the database. The librarians intend to add more fields to aid in finding the documents in the future and to improve searching capabilities. The number of keywords will be increased, and the searching options will be expanded so specific fields can be searched and limits can be placed. Show-all functions will be created for the original four categories, so a users can essentially browse the original ordering of the entries, which will allow them to catch records that they may miss with the search.

BENEFITS

The guide is already a great benefit to the library staff and, with future improvements, will become even easier to use. On February 15, 2005, the guide in the database format was made available to both Goddard Library librarians and the project librarians. For February, Web use statistics report the following:

91 page views, 85 user sessions, and 31 unique users. For March, the following was reported: 213 page views, 190 user sessions, and 34 unique users. Assessment of the guide is still in the early stages but the feedback so far indicates that the guide is a useful tool for accessing difficult-to-find information.

The Goddard Library has an intelligent, but very "junior," reference staff. The guide has aided them in their own personal exploration of the Goddard information landscape and has made it possible for them to contribute to it as well. The benefits of having Early's knowledge available in a written form can be summarized as follows:

1. *The knowledge can be more readily shared among a group of people rather than just benefiting a single individual.*
   When Early helps one of the staff with a question, only that staff member gains knowledge from the interaction. By compiling the knowledge in written form, all of the library staff will benefit because the resources necessary to answer the question will be at their fingertips. Not only will library staff benefit, but also the project librarians situated in many different locations on the Goddard campus. Where before only one person benefited, now dozens will benefit from Early's knowledge.

2. *Questions can be addressed in a timely manner.*
   Early is not always available when a patron calls for help. By taking a proactive approach, the staff are able to answer the patron's question quickly, even when Early is out of the office. Also, rather than spending hours making phone calls to discover where some archived information is stored (e.g., a print report from 20 years ago that hasn't been indexed anywhere), the staff can find the correct repository immediately.

3. *The* Goddard How To Get It Guide *will be the pooled knowledge of many brains, not just one.*
   The guide is not intended to represent just the experience of one reference librarian but to represent the experience of all the reference librarians as they learn and grow in their jobs and as information sources change or expand. Any one of the librarians can add an entry to the guide.

Different people have their own specialized knowledge to which everyone will now have access, and, thus, everyone will benefit.

CONCLUSION

The library now has a dynamic, ever-growing knowledge base, which will improve the reference services of the library and project libraries by increasing awareness of the many resources available to us, and will also provide a training tool for new staff members. The ability to record and share knowledge with colleagues, regardless of location, is of vital importance in a desktop work environment. Human and information resources are geographically distributed and connected through technology. The guide serves as a tool for collaboration as well as a repository of collective reference knowledge.

The e-mail reference transactions precariously stored in the outbox of Early's e-mail account turned out to be an irreplaceable representation of his knowledge and his work. The importance of the tangible artifacts created from virtual reference transactions will no doubt continue to be an important topic of study. The lesson learned for the Goddard Library, and perhaps for other libraries, is to take advantage of technology to preserve the valuable knowledge contained within virtual transactions.

The *Goddard How to Get it Guide* took several months and the work of six people to create. While the effort has truly been that of a team and will continue to be so, the guide could not exist without the knowledge and experience of Charles Early. The guide will be renamed in recognition of his work but also to better capture the functionality of the guide. Henceforth, the guide shall be known as the Cooperative Holistic Approach to Retrieving Literature in Engineering and Science, CHARLES.

NOTE

1. The database was designed by staff member Lee Goldblatt. The guide is built on an AMP open source platform. AMP is an acronym for the combined use of an Apache Web server, MYSQL relational database, and PHP scripting language. This platform was chosen as it is rapidly becoming the de facto standard for serving dynamic Web pages to users. The advantages

of AMP include a global-scale user base, open source licensing, stable and scalable structure, and easy migration. The global user base has created copious documentation, and this vast community supports fast development, quick resolution of technological bugs, and no re-inventing of the wheel. The scalability of the platform is assured as it was designed from the ground up to handle heavy Internet work loads. Easy migration is made possible as all popular operating systems are supported. Therefore, an organization could change from a Linux to a Solaris host and keep the same AMP implementation. For more information on the AMP platform, www.onlamp.com/.

REFERENCES

Doezema, June C., and Barbara J. Fox. 1998. *How to Get It: A Guide to Defense-Related Information Resources*. 6th ed. Fort Belvoir, VA: Defense Technical Information Center.

Gandhi, Smiti. 2004. "Knowledge Management and Reference Services." *The Journal of Academic Librarianship* 30, no. 5 (September): 368–381.

Gross, Madeline M. 2002. "Capturing Undocumented Worker-Job-Knowledge at Electric Utilities: The EPRI Strategic Project." New Century, New Trends. Proceedings of the 2002 IEEE 7th Conference on Human Factors and Power Plants (Cat. No. CH37335). Scottsdale, Arizona: IEEE: 6–24.

Hirsh, Sandra, and Jamie Dinkelacker. 2004. "Seeking Information in Order to Produce Information: An Empirical Study at Hewlett Packard Labs." *Journal of the American Society for Information Science and Technology* 55, no. 9: 807–817.

Hoffman, Robert R., and Lewis F. Hanes. 2003. "The Boiled Frog Problem." *IEEE Intelligent Systems* (July/August): 68–71.

Jantz, Ron. 2001. "Knowledge Management in Academic Libraries: Special Tools and Processes to Support Information Professionals." *Reference Services Review* 29, no. 1: 33–39.

Katz, William A. 2002. *Introduction to Reference Work*. 8th ed. 2 vols. Boston: McGraw-Hill.

Liebowitz, Jay. 2002. "Knowledge Management in a Large Government Organization." *Information and Knowledge Sharing: Proceedings of the IASTED International Conference*, St. Thomas Virgin Islands: 51–53.

"OCLC Acquires 24/7 Reference." (2004). *Library Journal* 129, no. 15 (September): 22.

Perez, Ernest. 1999. "Knowledge Management in the Library—Not." *Database* 22, no. 2 (April/May): 75–78.

Stover, Mark. 2004. "Making Tacit Knowledge Explicit: The Ready Reference Database as Codified Knowledge." *Reference Services Review* 32, no. 2: 164–173.

Chapter 9

Building Wi-Fi Technology and a New Mobile Service Model: Creating Change in Information Service Delivery at the Orange County (Florida) Library System

Kathryn Robinson

OVERVIEW

Communication, mobility, and maximizing staff resources are important elements in providing efficient, proactive customer service. The Orange County Library (Fl.) System is using 802.11 (b) compatible wireless technology, including videoconferencing, phones, and computers, to offer mobile service to respond to changing customer expectations and usage patterns. This mobile service is becoming our new service model. The use of lightweight communications badges utilizing voice recognition software has improved communications between staff. The use of wireless phones along with wireless computers has begun to free staff from the reference desk tether. Now staff from anywhere in the library, in the lobby, the stacks, the hallways can call ahead to other locations for customers, check the catalog, and place reserves, thereby taking service to the customer instead of requiring the customer to seek out a reference desk.

Self-contained videoconferencing units specifically designed for direct one-on-one communication, each with LCD screen, camera, and microphone, connect three branch locations and one department at Main with QuestLine, the Library's call center, thereby offering another option for customer assistance.

INTRODUCTION

Over the last few years we have been observing changes in statistics and trends at the Orange County Library System in Central Florida. We could see that while circulation was increasing and directional questions were up at the branches, reference questions were declining. This is a reflection of the trend nationwide. According to statistics compiled by the Association of Research Libraries, the median number of reference questions at member institutions peaked in 1997 and dropped 14% over the following four years. (Janes, 2003: 39) People's needs and expectations were changing and people had more options for finding information on their own. Both the use of computers and computer classes continued to grow in popularity. We found ourselves facing competition from online retail sellers of books, music, and movies as well as from local book stores with coffee, comfortable seating, and story times. And even greater competition came from the popularity of Google and from the fact that many, even though they may not be especially information literate, are satisfied with the information they find. Additional types of technology were becoming readily available and wireless technology particularly intrigued us. Our vision evolved into making the best use of our valuable staff resources to provide excellent customer service. It was about reinventing our work and our work flow to better meet the library mission of "Information, Imagination and Inspiration" in a way that was timely and convenient to our customers and cost effective for our tax payers.

BACKGROUND

The Orange County Library System has served the needs of the Central Florida community since the opening of Orlando's Albertson Public Library in 1923. Starting with a single location, the Orange County Library System has grown to include 14 additional branch locations within the county boundaries. The main library has 290,000 square feet and the branches range in size from 6,000 to 15,000 square feet. The system staff totals about 315 FTEs, and five of our locations are open seven days a week.

The Orange County Library System (OCLS) is a vibrant, innovative, and growing library system providing services to a population of 915,572 residents in Orange County. The population of Orange County doubled from 1980 to 2000. As one of the fastest growing counties in Florida, the population is expected to double again from the year 2000 to 2030 to a conservative estimate of 1.8 million. Of this projected growth, 63% is anticipated to be from people moving into the county and 56% of those are expected to be between 15 and 29 years old (Orange County Planning Division, 2004a). This rapid growth and increasingly diverse customer base is challenging the library to determine a realistic plan for continuing to provide efficient and convenient service options for rapidly increasing numbers of residents.

For 30 years OCLS has conducted an immensely popular home-delivery service that acts as a virtual branch and delivers as many as 60,000 items in a month. Programs for all ages and computer-based classes are provided at each library location. Each librarian in the system partners with two elementary schools so that we can become more a part of the community and reach out to children and their teachers and parents. Ten years ago OCLS separated phone and walk-in service at the main library, permitting staff to give more focused attention to

Table 9-1
Population Growth for Orange County, Florida

Year	Population of Orange County
1980	470,867
1990	677,491
2000	896,344
2004	1,013,937
2030, moderate projection	1,797,582

either the person in the library or the person on the phone. The phone service was named QuestLine. Eventually reference by e-mail was added to QuestLine, in 2003 we began to offer "Orange Chat" reference service, and in January 2004 we began to participate in the statewide Chat program, "Ask a Librarian." In April 2004 we began a videoconferencing service project named "OLIVE."

Gradually over a ten-year period, while walk-in traffic continued to grow, reference questions were decreasing. Since FY 92/93, a peak year for reference questions at OCLS, reference questions were on a downward trend system wide. Directional questions at main were declining, and directional questions were soaring at branches. Some of this is explained by the growth patterns in which 75% of the growth in Orange County between 1990 and 2000 has been in unincorporated areas (Orange County Planning Division, 2004a) and this trend is expected to continue. In FY 91/92 over 60% of all reference and directional questions were answered at main, and 10 years later 60% of the total are

Figure 9-1
Reference Questions Decline While Directional
Questions Increase

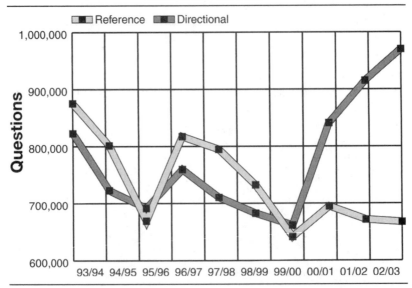

answered at the branches. While customer habits were changing, OCLS continued to provide the same or similar work routines and staffing patterns year after year. Eventually we realized that we needed to make changes and that new developments in technology were providing us with the opportunities to meet the changing needs and expectations of our rapidly growing and increasingly diverse population.

Clearly, the increase in technology options is having a dramatic impact in our lives and in how business is conducted. "More than six million American adults have listened to podcasts" from the web (Rainie and Madden, 2005: 1); "on a typical day, 13 million American adults use online banking (Fox, 2005: 1); and 53 million American adults report using instant messaging (Shiu and Lenhart, 2004: i). Lee Rainie (2005: 3), the founding director of the Pew Internet and American Life Project, reports that in one typical weekday, 41 million Americans use a search engine, more than 10 times the number of people who went to a public library. Similarly, Steve Coffman (Anhang and Coffman, 2002) writes that patrons have found the Web to be a much more convenient place than libraries for obtaining information, and using statistics from SearchEngine Watch (www.searchenginewatch.com/reports/perday.html) and the National Center for Education concluded: "People on the Web are doing almost as many searches per day as the total number of questions asked in libraries over the course of a full year" (p. 50). The availability of the Internet, search engines, and online

Table 9-2
Shift in Percentage of Questions Answered at Main
Over 60% of All Questions Answered at Main in FY 91/92,
10 Years Later about 40% Answered at Main

FY 01/02	Directional	Reference	Telephone	Walk in	Total
Main	29%	56%	74%	22%	41%
Branches	71%	44%	26%	78%	59%
FY91/92	Directional	Reference	Telephone	Walk in	Total
Main	54%	75%	74%	60%	64%
Branches	46%	25%	26%	40%	36%

databases has undoubtedly had an impact on library services as our customers are accessing Google, the library catalog, and remote access databases from home and from the office. In the library many customer requests are for basic computer assistance: how to sign up for a computer, getting started on a program, or troubleshooting a technical issue. Customers are conducting their own searches and are often not seeking help with locating quality sources. The Pew Internet and American Life Project reported recently (Fallows, 2005: i) that "92% of those using search engines are confident in their searching skills, 87% say they are usually successful in their searches and 68% believe search engines are a fair and unbiased source of information." In fact, the subtitle of the report is "Internet Searchers are Confident, Satisfied and Trusting—but They are also Unaware and Naïve." The proactive offering of individual customized assistance to show library users searching techniques and reliable sources allows librarians to compete with the Internet as a search tool.

In order to remain viable in this atmosphere of competition and changing expectations, libraries must market their services, make strong connections with the community, anticipate trends, and use new technology in ways to make services as timely and convenient as possible. And, as always, libraries, taking a role in information literacy, can offer added value to customers by helping them to define their information needs and connecting them in a timely manner with quality information and resources.

OCLS has a tradition of anticipating patron convenience and being responsive to customer needs with a "Here and Now" philosophy of customer service. Telephone reference (QuestLine), e-mail questions, chat reference, drive-up windows, home delivery of library materials (MAYL), online card registration, online credit card payments, electronic newsletters, streaming videos, and programs and classes at every location are examples of our efforts to set up services to meet customers' varying preferences for convenience of access. One of the newer developments in customer service is the development of OLIVE, OCLS Interactive Virtual Experience, which uses individual video-conferencing equipment between the three branch locations and the main library for an additional means of customer service. Other recent services include downloadable audio

Figure 9-2
Overall Reference Questions Declining While Directional Questions Soaring at Branches

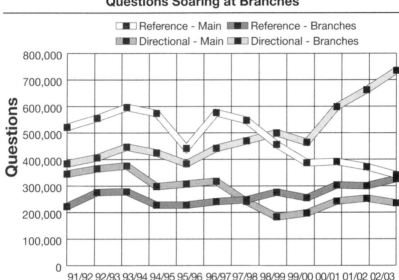

books, online classes and tutorials, streaming video of story-telling and booktalking, Really Simple Syndication (RSS) feeds to library news, a catalog that can be accessed by Palm Pilots™ and handheld PCs and with metasearching capabilities, a digitization history project (Central Florida Memory), and an overall increased focus on the creation of digital content.

We recognized that the proportion of in-house use of the library was shifting from the main library to the branch libraries. While reference interactions were down over all, the number of directional questions was increasing at branches. A shift in staffing towards the branches made it imperative to utilize staff resources at the Main library as efficiently as possible.

THE PHILOSOPHY: GETTING OUT FROM BEHIND THE REFERENCE DESK

While looking at our staffing and building organization at the main library, we realized that we had a large number of traditional reference desks to staff with a reduced number of inquiries. Before the availability of public Internet stations, library patrons headed straight to the reference desk upon arrival. When public-access computers were added in the mid-90s we experienced patrons rushing past the reference desks heading straight for the computers. It was clear that we were experiencing a major change; however it took some time to come to grips with what to do about it. It has been more difficult for some than for others to accept a change in roles and to let go of the "golden days" of reference. We have to accept that the Internet has so dramatically altered our customer-librarian relationship that "no effort to reassert a traditional library role can possibly succeed" (Wilson, 2000: 389).

On and off over the last decade we experimented some with "roving," which meant staff were assigned to work out on the floor and proactively offer assistance. Roving has been described as "point of need reference instruction" or "discovering reference questions that otherwise might never be asked . . ." and roving is credited with breaking "down barriers and limitations imposed by physical and mental reference 'desks'" (Fritch and Mandernack, 2001: 302). Information seekers typically prefer to conduct their own information searches (Stratigos and Strouse, 2003: 74), and with the trend towards self-service, patrons often don't discover they need some assistance until they are using the computers or until they are in the library stacks. Sometimes when working independently library users are unaware that they could receive better results with some staff guidance. When we began to offer assistance out on the floor instead of waiting at a desk for the customer, library users, unaccustomed to this more proactive offer of help, tended to be hesitant at first. We have found that it helps to be out and about on the floor, especially near the computers, making eye contact and being observant about who might be wandering around or using the computers and looking like they were lost. This gives us the opportunity to "play to our strengths" (Janes, 2002: 4) by assisting library visitors who perhaps have less-advanced computer or searching skills, evaluate which resources best meet their needs, and help them to conduct searches more effectively. Recently commenting on two different types of experiences, one working at a desk and the other working out on the floor, a new library intern wrote in her journal with some surprise that she actually was asked more questions out in the stacks than during the previous week when she was behind the reference desk.

To many library professionals, the reference desk as a place has become entwined with the notion of service. James Rettig (2002: 2) has written: "Reference service has been strongly associated with specific place. Our vocabulary—reference desk, reference room—has long reflected and reinforced this. . . . Inherent in both this practice and the design of our facilities has been the belief that they serve who sit and wait." Yet there has long been a recognition that this reliance on staff at a desk should change. Barbara J. Ford (1986: 491) wrote in 1986 that librarians must start "exploring alternatives and possibly eliminating the reference desk." Instead she envisioned that someday customers might give frequently asked questions and receive answers to these questions at a computer terminal. About the passive approach to reference service, in which we wait for customers to come to us instead of proactively helping customers when and where they need help, Anne Grodzins Lipow (2003: 31) wrote: "The reference desk was never a good idea ...standing behind a desk waiting for someone to say, 'I can't find what I'm looking for' . . . They have stood ready to help 'just in case' . . . reference service—in particular, point-of-need reference service has been an afterthought."

We started to refocus on reference not as a place but as a service that the library provides. Reference is not *where* we are assigned to work ("I'm on the desk") but rather the reference and directional assistance that we provide. The availability of wireless technology now frees staff from the mind-set that service must take place at a desk. Libraries have the unique opportunity to rethink operating methods. Managers are looking at statistics, technology, and innovations at other libraries and in other industries as part of the process of rethinking how we do our work. We read about the Cerritos (Calif.) Library's use of self-check-out and handheld computers (Spors, 2002) and heard about changes to the organization of reference collections and service at the Pittsburgh (Pa.) Public Library. We also followed the progress of the planning for the new Seattle (Wash.) Public

Figure 9-3
The "Before" Picture

Library. These developments inspired us and affirmed that we were headed in the right direction.

The addition of the wireless network at OCLS opened up many possibilities for rethinking the way we organize our workflow and provide reference service. Wireless technology gives us the ability to break tradition and move away from the desk; to no longer think of reference as a place but as a service. The old model of waiting at desk for someone to come and request assistance was declared obsolete. The new service model for in-house library users included proactively offering assistance, giving added-value services, and assisting from anywhere point in the building.

THE TECHNOLOGY: WIRELESS PHONES AND COMPUTERS

A series of projects needed to be completed in order to free staff from the reference-desk tether, the first of which was creating the wireless environment. The library installed an 802.11 (b) compatible wireless access system for staff use in 2003 (later for use by the public) and implemented trials of wireless communications units (Vocera devices) and wireless computers, including tablet PCs and pocket PCs. The Vocera trial improved communications from one floor to another, as these wearable units made access possible to an individual nearly anywhere in the building. This resulted in less reliance on a traditional phone system and a quicker response from staff when assistance was needed elsewhere in the building. The wireless computer trial made it possible to consult the library catalog in the

Figure 9-4
Use of Wireless Communication Badge for Customer Service

stacks, in the lobby, and anywhere assistance might happen to be needed. This is in keeping with Rettig's (2002: 4) value of "mobility."

The Vocera communications system (www.vocera.com) gives staff the ability to contact other employees within the main library via an 802.11(b) wireless device. This badge, which utilizes Nuance voice-recognition software, weighs just under two ounces and is worn around the neck on a lanyard or clipped onto a shirt collar, lapel, or pocket. With the push of a button staff can contact any other staff member wearing a badge, broadcast a message to all badge wearers, call phone extensions within the library, and access outside phone lines through the Vocera server and a Dialogics board that bridges the Vocera server to the library's PBX system. If there is a need for more staff at a given location, any staff member can be contacted and reallocated to that area. Employees can call from floor to floor to request materials housed elsewhere and can advise staff on another floor that a patron will be arriving with

Figure 9-5
Vocera Communications Network

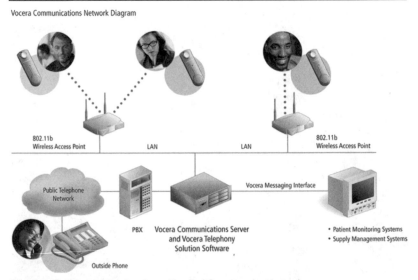

Vocera Communications Network Diagram

802.11b
Wireless Access Point   LAN   LAN   802.11b
Wireless Access Point

Public Telephone
Network   Vocera Messaging Interface

PBX   Vocera Communications Server
       and Vocera Telephony   • Patient Monitoring Systems
       Solution Software   • Supply Management Systems

Outside Phone

Reprinted with permission from Vocera Communications, Inc.

a certain type of request. The library has purchased sufficient Vocera units for each reference staff member on a shift at the main library.

Staff first experimented with using a tablet PC and a pocket PC. The wireless computers, along with the wireless phones began to free staff from the reference desk. Using these devices enables library staff to check the library catalog from anyplace, thereby taking additional customer service to the customer. The library was awarded the 2004 American Library Association (ALA) Loleta D. Fyan Grant which was used to purchase additional equipment; a handheld computer with keyboard, several pocket computers with thumb pads, and other pocket PCs that are used with a stylus. We now have pocket PCs in sufficient numbers so all staff on a shift can be equipped with both a portable computer device and a wireless phone device.

Figure 9-6
Use of PDAs in Service Delivery

THE TECHNOLOGY: OLIVE (OCLS INTERACTIVE
VIRTUAL EXPERIENCE)

The library purchased compact self-contained videoconferencing systems specifically designed for direct one-on-one communication. (The first units were purchased from Tandberg (www.tandberg.net/). The wireless units feature an LCD screen, camera, microphone, and telephone headset/handset. The first installation connected the library's busiest branch, Alafaya (13 miles from the main library and a monthly circulation of over 50,000 items), with QuestLine, the call center at the main library where queries are handled by phone, chat, e-mail and fax. The OLIVE unit, which is portable, is placed in QuestLine at one of the computer workstations so that staff have access to databases and the Internet for answering questions and so that they can perform other duties in between OLIVE calls. Trials on using video conferencing for patron assistance began in April 2004. Additional units have been installed at two other branch locations: one that is another busy branch and the second, a location with less traffic and more limited staffing. More recently OCLS has been experimenting with one additional OLIVE unit placed in a less busy area of the main library.

Before the start of videoconferencing, it was difficult to anticipate what types of assistance patrons would request using OLIVE. At first we believed that customers would be referred to QuestLine staff when branch staff had a more difficult question or when branch staff were busy. It turns out that people ask the same types of questions using OLIVE as they do in any face-to-face library transaction, anything from directional information about the library collection to library account information and reference questions. Often there are requests to find out if the main library has a specific title that is not currently available at the branch location.

Managers, librarians, and support staff have all answered OLIVE. Much of the time support staff most ably handle these requests. While it was anticipated that some formal staff training would be needed prior to using OLIVE, we have learned that staff who answer phones in QuestLine were readily able to assist patrons with OLIVE. It really is little different from helping a

Figure 9-7
QuestLine Manager Using OLIVE and Online Resources
to Assist Customers

patron on the phone except that you have the added benefit of seeing each other. One immediate lesson for staff, already experienced in answering requests by phone, was to remember that all facial expressions, body language, and movements, such as walking towards the OLIVE unit, were clearly visible to the library customer on the branch screen the moment the branch customer picked up the receiver.

OLIVE was first opened for service with no announcement or publicity of any kind. While a logo for OLIVE has been created and the service is available at multiple locations, the service still has not been advertised. This has allowed library staff time to see how the technology works, see how patrons respond, and become accustomed to this new service. A more recent development is the addition of software that will allow main staff

Figure 9-8
The Customer's View of OLIVE

to push pages on the OLIVE screen to the library customers who are being assisted at the branches. Design of a new shell for housing OLIVE units is being considered. It would be advantageous to have something attractive that draws people to it, while still sturdy and practical.

When customers first see the equipment, their reactions range from intimidation to curiosity or excitement. The first few months there were many hang-ups as the curious (many were children) who picked up the receiver at the branch location were startled by immediately seeing and hearing a staff member on the screen. Sometimes staff were asked, "Are you a real person?" or "Are you OLIVE?" Once customers have used OLIVE, the responses are uniformly positive. Because the screen image is so clear and the movements appear instantaneous, OLIVE does give the feeling of a personal face-to-face service transaction. We have experimented with and have hopes of someday being able to offer access to service from home and from other points in the community to a combination of chat and videoconferencing.

REORGANIZATION: CHANGING THE WORK FLOW

How do libraries ensure sufficient time for librarians to update Web pages, develop online tutorials, market the library to the community; to have the time to create and present programs and classes, to do community outreach, and to participate in chat reference? And how do library managers create the possibility of call centers so that main staff take phone requests for information and materials from branch patrons? The best use needs to be made of each staff person's time. Work flow must be streamlined and staff must become more in tune with customer service as a guiding principal rather than as something that occurs at a place: the reference desk.

We recognized that our past practice had been to be at staff locations "just in case" (Lipow, 2003: 31), or, in other words, in anticipation of what the demand might be. We decided to streamline the workflow so staff would perform different aspects of information service. One mobile team member could greet and accompany patrons to stacks as well as pull titles and simple subject requests. Another person could work on face-to-face requests and on more difficult questions about which customers needed to be called back. Other staff could help throughout the building with general directional assistance. Having trained clerical staff do more routine functions, such as doing catalog checks, pulling title requests, answering account questions, and providing directional information, allowed librarians more opportunity for creating digital content, for providing programs and classes, for participating in community outreach all in addition to answering reference questions. With the use of wireless technology staff can be more mobile and the numbers and the locations of staff can be fluid to adapt to where and when patrons need assistance. This has been described in a variety of ways, such as "right here, right now" (Stratigos and Strouse, 2003), "point of need reference instruction" (Fritch and Mandernack, 2001: 302) and "point-of-need reference service" (Lipow, 2003: 31).

The traditional manner of managing reference service at OCLS had been that department heads were responsible for subject areas such as arts and literature, business and science, social science, genealogy, law, children's and telephone reference. We reorganized both the circulating print collection and reference materials into straight Dewey order. This created a more intuitive arrangement for those library users who prefer self-service. Popular materials, fiction and audiovisual formats, were relocated to Library Central, the remodeled first-floor area, with face-out display shelving for DVDs, CDs, and best sellers.

At the same time the collection was rearranged, the management structure for reference services was adjusted. Instead of managers being responsible for subject areas, most became responsible for types of service delivery or work flow: walk-in service, remote service, follow-up reference, as well as programs and services for children and teens. Managing by process rather than by Dewey subject areas also led to the need for a manager of the day, or MOD, to monitor the overall daily work flow. Staff are scheduled to work anywhere in the division and so cross-training was provided. The training program for librarians was called "Share Your Skills." Each librarian created training for other staff on specific topics. First the materials were shared in a classroom setting. Then the information was used to create streaming videos for any interested staff to view from the staff intranet. An additional training program for library clerks called "Ready, Set, Go" was provided. The content, which included determining customer needs and library resources and policies, was provided via an online course followed up by classroom sessions and a participant blog.

Reference Central

Instead of reference desks throughout the building in different subject areas, the main library at OCLS now has one main reference area, called Reference Central. Librarians answer questions, locate resources, and assist customers in the use of print and electronic resources. Patrons either walk into Reference Central independently or are accompanied there by mobile staff.

QuestLine and QuestLine II

"Remote" reference service, by phone, fax, e-mail, chat, and video-conferencing, is provided by QuestLine. Calls to 6 branches, and soon for all 14 branch locations, will be directed through Quest-Line, thereby making it a true call center for the entire library system. Phone vectoring makes it possible to use both librarians and reference clerks as queries can be directed by the type of question and the staff needed to answer the question. Through QuestLine patrons may ask questions, request titles, reserve or renew items, and manage their library accounts. Materials can be held at the drive-up window or book return, or they can be delivered by a courier service. In 90% of the QuestLine requests, the questions are answered in QuestLine with the patron remaining on the phone. The other 10% are entered into a database and are automatically printed out in the QuestLine II location where the questions are divided into reference questions and basic subject or title requests to be allotted to the appropriate staff to complete.

Mobile Assistance

Mobile staff greet customers in the lobby or anywhere in the building and may accompany customers throughout the building as needed. This was started with a few staff who volunteered to experiment with being mobile, and over time other staff have asked to participate. The first volunteers kept journals of their mobile experience, which helped identify the areas in which training was needed and helped us learn how the service differs in actual use from what we had anticipated. Mobile staff seek out patrons who look like they need help. They approach customers entering the library or a department and approach library users at catalog/database stations and offer help. They assist in developing search strategies and can help identify reliable resources. They place holds on library materials; call ahead to other locations for the customer, getting materials retrieved and brought to the customer from another floor; and verify the best place in the building to refer the patron when a referral is needed. Staff also use these interactions as opportunities to market the library and let customers know about other services

Figure 9-9
Greeting and Determining the Customer's Needs

of which they may be unaware. For example, someone searching on a particular subject could be told about an upcoming
class, program, or online tutorial on a related topic. This adds
value to the information the customer is seeking and markets
the library as the place to come for meeting information needs.
The goal is to eventually have all customer-service staff flexible
and wireless and moving about when and where needed to provide the best possible customer service.

CONCLUSION: A "WORK IN PROGRESS"

In 2000 the largest population by generation group in Orange
County, Florida, was baby boomers. However, by 2005 and

Figure 9-10
Walk-in and Virtual Service is a Work in Progress

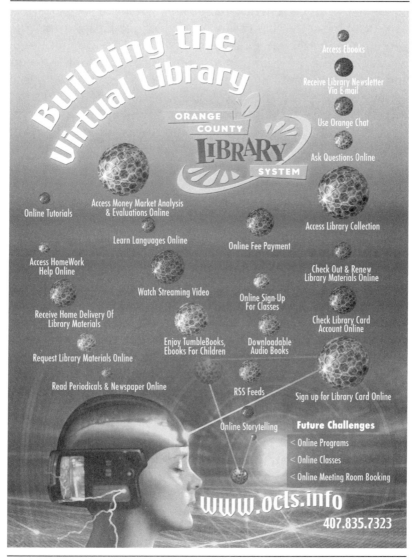

through 2030 it is projected that the largest population group
will be the Generation Y, those born between 1977 and 1994
(Orange County Planning Department, 2004b: 12). We must

continue to make changes to meet the needs and expectations of the technology-savvy Generation Y, while still addressing the needs of the other generational groups. We have to be diligent about looking at the changes in technology and figuring out how to continue to apply new technology to enhance customer service, surveying our community members as to what they need and expect, and continuing to observe trends in the market place using resources such as www.trendwatching.com. I often have heard managers explain to customers and staff alike that we, not just OCLS, but the library community itself is a "work in progress." We are constantly changing, but technology is evolving so rapidly that new possibilities are constantly being created. We expect to be a "work in progress" for the foreseeable future.

We have long accepted that the traditional desk can be a barrier to patrons requesting assistance. Despite this knowledge, it is difficult to change long-term practices. Perhaps it is easier to make changes when constructing a new facility than it is to make changes to a structure and a culture that has been in place for a number of years. In recent years, as OCLS has begun to change the location, size, look, and number of service points in a building that was constructed in 1985, we were asking both customers and staff to let go of something with which they have had nearly 20 years of success and familiarity. It takes time for both the public and staff to adapt to the changes. For some staff it is challenging to let go of the routine and work flow which has become second nature. Some customers desire the assurance of a service point so they know for sure where to go to get assistance while others are excited about having customer service delivered in the way most convenient to them. Besides our more efficient work flow the best part of all the more recent changes has been the positive public response. Often customers express surprise and delight at both the wireless technology and the proactive service. While there is a bit of an adjustment in changing the look of the library by gradually removing the traditional desks, there is also a clear appreciation for the attentiveness to the customers needs.

About the future library, Stratigos and Strouse (2003: 76) wrote: "Future libraries will provide information to users wherever they are, from wherever the information is." In library assistance we have started on that road with the purchase of portable computers, wireless communication devices, and one-on-one videoconferencing equipment for customer assistance. We have also forged ahead in the virtual customer service arena with online tutorials, storytelling by streaming video, electronic newsletters, and RSS Feeds. We are still nearer the beginning of this journey. We know some parts of the trip will be easier and some bumpier. We know neither what is ahead nor all that we will learn along the way. We are glad for the opportunity to continue to play a role in connecting customers visiting the library—both in person and virtually—to information and materials, and we are excited by the adventure ahead.

REFERENCES

Anhang, Abe, and Steve Coffman. 2002. "The Great Reference Debate." *American Libraries* 33, no. 3 (March): 50–54.

Fallows, Deborah. 2005. "Search Engine Users." Pew Internet Project (January 23), www.pewinternet.org/reports.asp (accessed September 8, 2005).

Ford, Barbara J. 1986. "Reference beyond (and without) the Reference Desk." *College & Research Libraries* 47 (September): 491–494.

Fox, Susannah. 2005. "Online Banking 2005," Pew Internet Project Data Memo, www.pewinternet.org;/reports.asp (accessed April 7, 2005).

Fritch, John W., and Scott B. Mandernack. 2001. "The Emerging Reference Paradigm: A Vision of Reference Services in a Complex Information Environment." *Library Trends* 50, no. 2 (Fall): 286–305.

Janes, Joseph. 2003. *Introduction to Reference Work in the Digital Age*. New York: Neal-Schuman.

Janes, Joseph. 2002. "What is Reference For?" The Future of Reference Services Paper presented at the American Library Association Annual Conference in Atlanta, GA, www.ala.org/rusa/rusaprotools/futureofref/whatref.htm (accessed June 11, 2004).

Lipow, Anne Grodzins. 2003. "The Future of Reference: Point-of-Need Reference Service: No Longer an Afterthought." *Reference Services Review* 31, no. 1: 31–35. Future of Reference Services Paper presented at the 2002 ALA Annual Conference in Atlanta, www.ala.org/rusa/rusaprotools/futureofref/pointofneed.htm (accessed June 11, 2004).

Orange County Planning Division, Research and Economic Development Section. 2004. "Orange County, Florida Population Projections Summary" (April), www.orangecountyfl.net/cms/DEPT/growth/planning/programs/researcheco/default.htm (accessed June 11, 2004).

Orange County Planning Division, Research and Economic Development Section. 2004. "Population Study Population Projections 2005-2030." Full report, www.orangecountyfl.net/cms/DEPT/growth/planning/programs/researcheco/default.htm (accessed October 21, 2005).

Raine, Lee. 2005. "Who Uses the Internet, What They Do, and What It Means."
    Presentation to the Freedom to Connect Conference (March 30), http://
    www.pewinternet.org/presentation_archive.asp (accessed April 7, 2005).
Raine, Lee, and Mary Madden. 2005. "Podcasting Catches On." Pew Internet
    Project Memo (April), www.pewinternet.org/reports.asp (accessed April
    7, 2005).
Rettig, James. 2002. "Technology, Cluelessness, Anthropology, and the Memex:
    The Future of Academic Reference Service." Future of Reference Services
    Paper presented at the American Library Association Annual Conference
    in Atlanta, www.ala.org/rusa/rusaprotools/futureofref/technology-
    cluelessness.htm (accessed June 5, 2004).
Shiu, Eulynn, and Amanda Lenhart. 2004. "How Americans Use Instant Mes-
    saging." Pew Internet Project Report (September 1), www.pew inter-
    net.org/reports.asp (accessed April 7, 2005).
Spors, Kelly K. 2002. "Libraries Focus on New Technology: After Adding
    Sofas, Coffee Bars, Public Libraries Turn to Tech." Wall Street Journal
    online article (January 10), www.msnbc.com/news/. No longer available
    on MSNBC Web site.
Stratigos, Anthea, and Roger Strouse. 2003. "Library of the Future." Online 3,
    no. 1 (January-February): 74–76.
Wilson, Myoung C. 2000. "Evolution or Entropy? Changing Reference/User
    Culture and the Future of Reference Librarians." Reference and User Ser-
    vices Quarterly 39, no. 4 (Summer): 387–390.

Chapter 10

Building a Virtual Community: Repurposing Professional Tools for Team-Based Experiential Learning

Karen Wenk

OVERVIEW

Rutgers University is creating a virtual collaboratory using professional open source publishing and conference software repurposed to create an experiential learning environment. This novel Web space functions as a laboratory and space for collaboration between interdisciplinary teams of partners working together. Teams include students and industry partners working with several departments, institutes, and librarians at the university. The collaboratory also uses Web-based tools such as chat, e-mail, videoconferencing, and shared calendars to facilitate synchronous and asynchronous communication among partners across time and distance. The collaboratory will be used in the keystone course of a new degree program, Food and Nutrition Business.

INTRODUCTION

This chapter will focus on the building of a novel environment—a virtual collaboratory[1] at Rutgers University that will serve as laboratory, meeting place, and work space for a new course called Food and Nutrition Business Informatics and Communication. The interdisciplinary team of partners in this endeavor at Rutgers University is made up of several Cook College departments and centers along with the Rutgers University Libraries and the School of Communication, Information and Library Studies. Students from the Department of Food Science, Nutritional Sciences and Agricultural and Resource Economics will work with New Jersey businesses and other organizations in this multidisciplinary environment. Each team's goal will be to develop a plan or proposal that can later be carried out in a real field experience or internship.

The virtual collaboratory will provide the technological infrastructure for the course, which will be the keystone for a new combined BS/MS program in Food Business. The course takes a creative and nontraditional approach to collaborative learning by involving members of the business community directly in the classroom-learning environment. This nontraditional learning experience requires a nontraditional learning space, the virtual collaboratory. The impetus for this course is the need to develop leaders who can work effectively with both science and business colleagues.

THE COURSE DESCRIPTION

Food and Nutrition Business Informatics and Communication is a new course that will be offered at Rutgers University for the first time in the spring semester of 2006. This course will provide a multidisciplinary approach to information literacy and real-world problem solving, as well as helping to build communication and teamwork skills in the context of food and nutrition business-information studies. The course is nontraditional in that much of the learning occurs outside of the classroom in a collaborative Web environment. The nature of the partnership between university members (faculty, librarians, and students) and industry makes the constraints of a classroom schedule problematic. The collaboratory is designed to mitigate the communication difficulties inherent in a team with diverse schedules and locations.

PARTNERS

The academic partners participating in this course form a team of educators from these departments and centers:

- Food Science and Nutritional Science Departments
- Agricultural, Food, and Resource Economics Department
- School of Communication, Information and Library Studies
- Rutgers University Libraries
- Center for Advanced Food Technology at Cook College
- Rutgers Food Policy Institute
- Food Innovation Center

Industry representatives will participate in the course on a very important level. They bring their business needs and problems into the classroom and allow the diverse team of students to help them reach their goals. The students benefit greatly by participating in real situations.

IMPETUS FOR CREATING THE COURSE

There were several factors that motivated and facilitated the creation of this course. The development of a new BS/MS degree program in food business illuminated the need for greater information literacy in the combined areas of food science, nutritional science, and business. The course is a natural outgrowth of several existing infrastructure elements at Rutgers and in the state at large. The university's Cook College has a cooperative education program that has strong relationships with small businesses that might participate. The Food Innovation Center and the Rutgers Food Policy Institute both provide a natural support system for the course. With a large food industry in place, which includes many small businesses and start-ups, New Jersey provides both an important source of employment for Rutgers graduates and a source of ready consumers for the cooperative assistance the course and new degree program offer. Program graduates will enter the workforce with a sound background in both food sciences and business. Critical skills needed include awareness of food science and nutrition research trends, business information for marketing and competitive intelligence, Geographic Information Systems (GIS) and census data for selecting locations for new enterprises, and knowledge of food safety and regulatory information.

STRUCTURE OF THE COURSE

The Informatics and Communication class meets in person in a traditional classroom setting on a regular 16-week semester schedule, just like any regular undergraduate class. The curriculum contains a very well-defined, team-taught, multidisciplinary schedule of learning modules that culminate in the development of a research project: formulating a research problem, devising an appropriate research plan, appropriate methods of research and data mining, and effective methods of communicating research to others. Faculty members from the participating departments teach selected sections of the course relevant to their expertise. Librarians introduce concepts dealing with information retrieval, evaluation, and effective communication of information.

Small groups of students will work together to form each team. Each team will consist of students from the participating disciplines: food science, nutritional science, business, and library and information science. These students will work together with an industry partner, who will provide a real-life problem for the team to solve. The final project, or deliverable, might be anything from a business plan to a new food additive.

Course Objectives

The objectives of the course are to

- develop a problem statement dealing with a real-world industry need.
- create a detailed action plan to follow up on the problem.
- learn effective information-seeking and data-mining skills.
- learn to critically evaluate information in terms of authenticity, bias, accuracy, and currency.

- develop effective communication skills across disciplines.
- allow students to work directly with industry partners.
- provide the opportunity for students to gain experience in the peer-review process

BUILDING THE VIRTUAL COLLABORATORY

The Food Nutrition and Business Informatics and Communication Virtual Collaboratory uses freely available open source applications in a unique and new combination. The multidisciplinary nature of the course and the variety of participants, many outside the university itself, have been the impetus to develop this new concept. The virtual collaboratory provides the technological infrastructure that creates the environment for active experiential learning that is an essential and integral part of the course. Industry partners provide real-life problems for teams of students to work on, which along with advice and mentorship by teaching faculty and librarians forms a virtual learning community. In addition, the virtual collaboratory simulates an actual professional environment complete with opportunities for publishing and developing conference presentations.

The collaboratory has several elements that are already familiar to most students. Forums, or bulletin boards, are available to provide asynchronous communication between students in each team, between individual teams, and between students and faculty as well as their business partners. The collaboratory uses online chat with Web cams for synchronous communication in any combination. These online chats can be scheduled via the integrated course calendar as well as e-mail. The calendar module of the collaboratory includes individual calendars for each team as well as a main calendar for the course.

The novel aspect of this virtual collaboratory is the use of open source online journal management, publishing, and conference systems. The Public Knowledge Project (PKP),[2] based at the University of British Columbia and led by John Willinski (2003) as principal investigator, has developed several open source systems; two of these systems are used in the virtual collaboratory and are described here. The Open Journal System (OJS) has been repurposed to provide the necessary collaborative environment for the course. OJS is a freely available, open source publishing system that allows authors to submit abstracts, upload their papers and supporting documents, and then interact with peer reviewers and editors in an easily customizable online environment. Collaboratory designers have adapted this software to provide a working support structure for students, industry partners, teaching faculty, and librarians to work as both editors and peer reviewers. Teams of students take the role of authors within the journal platform environment. Fellow classmates act as peer reviewers and comment on each other's projects. The teaching faculty and librarians, with the support and input of the industry partners, take on the job of editors. The final "publications" of the students' work at the end of the semester are archived for use as models in subsequent classes. The archive of student work, however, does not take advantage of the OJS software platform's internal final publication feature, which allows for viewing of past issues of an online journal. Because of the proprietary nature of some of the work done by students for their small business partners, the archive of papers will be available to a limited audience, with company names or other sensitive information masked.

The experience that students will gain in using the OJS feature of the virtual collaboratory is valid and relevant. Online publishing is gaining in popularity and use. As far back as 2001, Tenopir and King (2001) reported that more than 1,000 peer-reviewed journals were already being published in electronic-only format. Certainly, online submission and review, even for print journals, is commonplace,[3] thus making the experience of using the OJS for our course useful for the student's future work in a professional environment.

The flavor and atmosphere of a professional conference is not normally part of the academic classroom setting. To add another dimension to the experiential aspect of this program, we have included an end-of-semester conference as another component of the course. The virtual collaboratory provides a space for this conference. Students develop online poster sessions and participate in a "virtual conference" as a part of their final project presentations using Open Conference Software (OCS), the second component of the Public Knowledge Project's open source software. OCS allows the creation of a customized Web site for the virtual conference, a schedule for presentations, a call for papers (in this case a mandatory class assignment), registration of participants (students), and electronic submission of abstracts. The software has been repurposed in a way similar to that of the OJS in that the final conference, with its "published proceedings," is the output of the students' semester projects. Poster sessions will allow colleagues (fellow classmates) and industry partners to view and comment on all of the projects. Collaboration with industry partners in the classroom along with the opportunity to participate in a professional setting with members of the business community will enrich the total learning experience that the course provides.

The virtual collaboratory was developed using only open source software for several reasons. The benefits of using open-source software extend far beyond the obvious financial considerations. Open-source applications allow the kind of customizing that is not possible within the confines of most commercially available software. Having access to the program code allows modification of the interface to fit this unique application. Another benefit of using open-source software is that modified components can be made into an integrated reusable platform for use in other settings. The repurposing of the Open Journal System of publishing and the Open Conference System to fit the needs of collaborative learning is an innovation.

All of the components that have been detailed here are the individual building blocks that, much like the blocks of a building's foundation, support the virtual collaboratory. It is the Web space within which collaborative, experiential learning can occur between university students, faculty, and librarians along with industry partners from the greater community. The structure of communication between students, faculty, librarians, and business partners can be seen in Figure 10-1.

ASSESSMENT

The first stage in the development of this course is beta testing through a case study. This phase of development is already underway. A sample case study is currently being done using a local soup kitchen as the hypothetical business partner. The

Figure 10-1
Communication within the Virtual Collaboratory

Students &
Partners

New Ideas &
Opportunities

VIRTUAL
COLLABORATORY
• Library Resources
• Data Sets and Tools
• Publishing and Conference
• Collaboration Tools
  Synchronous and
  Asynchronous

Coursework
Teamwork

Informatics &
Communication

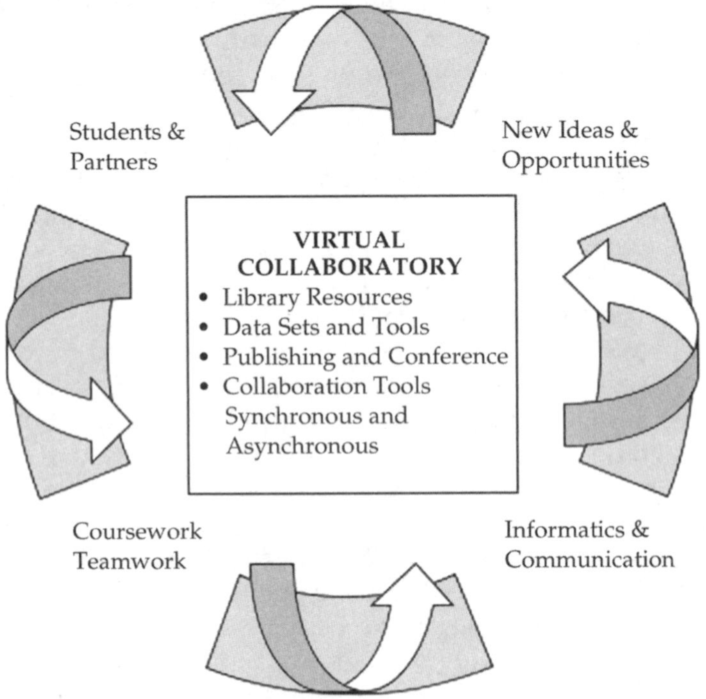

graduate students and faculty members who are creating the course are the participants in this phase. A successful outcome of the beta test will serve to validate the course curriculum and benefit the soup kitchen at the same time.

Once the beta-testing phase is completed, the course designers will develop an assessment evaluation plan to allow for ongoing feedback and modification of the curriculum in order to best meet the needs of industry partners and students. Pre- and post-test assessments of student learning will also be conducted.

CONCLUSION

The virtual collaboratory at Rutgers University is a novel "space" for teamwork and experiential learning. It is a powerful tool for the multidisciplinary framework of Rutgers' new course in Food and Nutrition Business Informatics and Communication, allowing for collaboration among partners with varied schedules, working in disparate locations.

The designer's repurposing of open source software provides an inexpensive and powerfully flexible platform for the course. Students' ability to work with a diverse team of individuals, gain valuable experience solving real-world problems and participate in a professional conference and publishing environment will help train skilled and flexible leaders for New Jersey's food-business sector.

The many technological advantages of working in the virtual collaboratory environment are examples of the usefulness of repurposing existing tools and technology to fit the needs of today's demanding educational programs.

NOTES

1. A collaboratory is a "'center without walls,' in which the nation's researchers can perform their research without regard to geographic location—interacting with colleagues, accessing instrumentation, sharing data and computational resources, [and] accessing information in digital libraries." Bill Wulf. (1989). http://collaboratory.emsl.pnl.gov/presentations/talk3.96/pg6.html (accessed October 13, 2004).
2. The Public Knowledge Project is involved in "the use of online infrastructure and knowledge management strategies to improve both the scholarly quality and public accessibility and coherence of this body of knowledge in a sustainable and globally accessible form," www.pkp.ubc.ca/about/what.html (accessed October 13, 2004).
3. Many major publishers prefer manuscripts be submitted online. As an example, Elsivier provides an "Author Gateway" for submitting papers to over 1,000 journals and tracking their progress through to the published article.

REFERENCES

Tenopir, Carol, and Donald W. King. 2001. "Lessons for the Future of Journals." *Nature* 413 no. 6857 (October 18): 672–673,
Willinsky, J. 2003. "The Nine Flavours of Open Access Scholarly Publishing." *Journal of Postgraduate Medicine* [serial online] 49: 263–267; www.jpgmonline.com/article.asp?issn=0022-3859;year=2003;volume=49;issue=3; spage=263;epage=267;aulast=Willinsky (accessed October 13, 2004).

Conclusion:

Looking to the Future

Marilyn Domas White

As an innovation in responding to users' information needs, digital reference in various forms has been around for a while, moving from the early, non-library-based ask-a-question services designed primarily for the K-12 community to a widely accepted service provided as well by public, academic, and special libraries, serving a broad community of users. In 2000, 45% (63 libraries) of a sample of 140 libraries in academic institutions emphasizing undergraduate and master's level education[1] had adopted digital reference (White, 2002); five years later, the adoption rate had increased to 76% (107 libraries). In 1999, 96% of larger research libraries primarily based in major research universities had adopted digital reference in some form[2] (Goetsch, 1999). Based on Everett Rogers' model (1995) of the diffusion of innovation, acceptance at these levels means that, in terms of the rate of diffusion, libraries in institutions emphasizing undergraduate and masters' level degrees were in the late majority stage, and the research libraries were at the laggards' stage in 1999.[3] It is only natural that, as digital reference becomes more common among libraries, the nature of research, discussion, and ideas related to its provision change. Case studies describing how digital reference was initially implemented in an individual library and providing early usage statistics naturally give way to studies covering more libraries and focusing on topics related to efficiency, effectiveness, and quality of service; needed systemic changes; behavioral changes influenced by media; and the value of human intermediation in an electronic environment.

In August 2002, 20 researchers from library science, digital libraries, and computer science met to develop a research agenda in digital reference. Their objectives were to identify significant problem areas and questions and, in general, to stimulate research that would bridge digital reference, library practice, and digital libraries. Organized by the Information Institute of Syracuse (N.Y.) University, the symposium was co-sponsored by the Association of College and Research Libraries, OCLC, the Harvard Graduate School of Education, and two national libraries: the Library of Congress and the National Library of Canada. David Lankes summarized the discussions and developed the digital reference research agenda more formally (Lankes 2004). He presented the agenda in a matrix of five major topics: human expertise, efficiency and effectiveness; information systems; questions; and answers, with 11 subtopics as rows and four conceptual lenses as columns: policy, systems, evaluation, and behavior (Lankes, 2004, Table 1). The agenda appeared in print probably too late to influence the papers submitted for this conference overtly, but, for purposes of looking at the nature of research as represented in the published conference proceedings, the agenda provides a useful framework.

At this stage of the development of digital reference, what elements of that research agenda are addressed in the chapters of this book?[4] The number of papers focusing on agenda items and their concentration of interests in agenda items may reflect the broader community's perception of the relative importance of the research questions addressed in the agenda. If there is relatively little overlap, then that finding is ambiguous. It can be interpreted as signs of the incompleteness of the agenda or as indications that the agenda has yet to be completely incorporated into the thinking of people writing about digital reference. The latter would not be surprising, considering that the agenda was not published until February 2004. Because the Virtual Reference Desk (VRD) conference theme in 2004 was broadened to reference in the future, an additional possibility is that some papers legitimately need not relate to this agenda at all.

In a very loose categorization, many of the chapters in this volume fit into the categories and research questions established in the agenda.

Paper	Broad area	Specific area
Early, Japson, Endres & Goldblatt	Human expertise	Systems
Hutchison & Pye	Efficiency and effectiveness	Cost
Daugaard, Fogh & Nielsen	Information system	Interoperability
Abels & Ruffner	Information system	System components
Blonde	Information system	System components
Robinson	Information system	System components
Radford	Questions	Reference interview

Note: Table is arranged by order of area in Digital Reference Research Agenda in Lankes (2004).

Three chapters do not fit easily into the schema, even allowing for very loose matches. What do these say about the agenda? Scott Nicholson and R. David Lankes' chapter undergirds many of the components in the agenda because they discuss the development of a resource that can provide data for addressing many of these questions. The chat transcripts in the warehouse, for example, would allow researchers to address questions related to the reference interview, such as assessing the current state of practice and determining the appropriate makeup of digital aids to help users formulate their questions. Reflecting the broader orientation of the conference, Karen Wenk's chapter on designing a collaboratory for a course at Rutgers, for example, involves reference librarians but emphasizes peer appraisal and communication by end users. As a result, it is not surprising that it does not fit into the agenda. Neither of these calls for any adjustment to the agenda itself.

The fact that the chapter on teenagers by Laura Kortz, Sharon Morris, and Louise W. Greene does not find an easy home does suggest that something is missing in the agenda.

What the authors have done is to look at a particular user group in some depth. The chapter characterizes the user group in terms of behavior and cognitive development and draws from that analysis an understanding of why and how that user group uses chat reference. Understanding and being able to predict the preference of different groups for various modes of delivering digital reference is a research topic of merit that does not seem to be included currently in the agenda and should be added.

Underlying this exercise of categorizing the chapters according to the agenda's framework are several objectives. The first is to test how well the agenda mirrors perceptions of the broader community. It is always possible for a small group of individuals to generate ideas that reflect their own interests and miss others that may be equally as important to others. Looking at the relationship between current published writing on digital reference and the agenda is a useful test. This sample of book is ideal for doing this because the contents are not likely to have been affected by publication of the agenda. After the agenda's publication, research may be influenced by the questions it suggests. Based on this small sample of papers and on a loose categorization of the papers, the agenda indeed matches the perception of people sufficiently interested in digital reference to write papers about it.

The second is to see if the agenda is complete. Has it actually identified all the topics and research questions that are important to digital reference? In this case, the analysis suggests that the agenda needs to incorporate at least one additional question or topic: understanding the rationale for a user's choice of alternative media for obtaining reference assistance. It is possible that other areas equally important have not yet been identified. Researchers and practitioners in digital reference need to consider the agenda as a working document subject to discussion and change as digital reference moves forward.

The third objective is the most important. It is to point to the merits of the agenda for focusing continued research in digital reference. Not only do researchers and practitioners in digital reference need to talk about the agenda, they need to use it as a map for research in the field. Yes, most of the papers in this volume address topics in the agenda, but they are not always focusing as precisely as they could on research questions that will move knowledge and practice on digital reference forward. And, when they do, they are not always using rigorous research methods that will ensure the most accurate results. With such a wide-spread service and with so few researchers and practitioners doing research, the community needs to work in a more concerted way to address key research questions, issues, and concerns. Answering the research questions posed in the agenda is essential to sharpening both the understanding and practice of digital reference and ensuring its success as an important means of meeting the information needs of people in the 21st century.

NOTES

1. These libraries are in Carnegie Foundation Masters Comprehensive Universities and Colleges (1994), Categories I and II, as defined in *The Carnegie Classification of Institutions of Higher Education*. Academic institutions in these categories offer undergraduate and master's degrees, but not doctorates; the categories vary by the number of master's degrees granted and the number of fields for those degrees. A new edition of this classification was published in 2000 after data collection in White's original study (2002). Definitions of the two categories differ slightly in wording between editions but not in content. The 2000 edition is available at: www.carnegie-foundation.org/Classification/index.htm (accessed May 26, 2005).
2. Lori Goetsch (1999) surveyed libraries who are members of the Association of Research Libraries.
3. Everett Rogers identifies adopter categories based on the time of adoption. The adopter categories are innovators, early adopters, early majority, late majority, and laggards, corresponding roughly to diffusion stages characterized by acceptance by 2.5%, 16%, 50%, 84%, and 100% of the potential adopters (Rogers, 1995: 262).
4. Not all papers were submitted for the proceedings volume, and not all papers submitted were selected. The papers then are truly selective, on the part of both the potential authors and the editors. In several instances related to non-submission, expanded versions of the papers have been or are being submitted to other professional publications.

REFERENCES

Carnegie Foundation for the Advancement of Teaching. 1994. *The Carnegie Classification of Institutions of Higher Education*. Menlo Park, CA: Carnegie Foundation for the Advancement of Teaching.

Goetsch, L. 1999. *Electronic Reference Services* (Spec Kit no. 251). Washington, DC: Association of Research Libraries.

Lankes, R. D. 2004. "The Digital Reference Research Agenda." *Journal of the American Society for Information Science and Technology* 55, no. 4: 301–311.

Rogers, E. 1995. *Diffusion of Innovations* (4th ed). New York: The Free Press.

White, M. D. 2002. "Diffusion of an Innovation: Digital Reference Service in Carnegie Foundation Master's (Comprehensive) Academic Institution Libraries." *Journal of Academic Librarianship* 27, no. 2: 173–187.

Index

A

Abels, Eileen G., 44, 49–72, 95,
    108, 205
    on evaluation, 26
    on industry standards, 94
Abram, Stephen, 6, 20
adolescent development, 5, 7
Agricultural, Food, and Resource
    Economics Department
    (Rutgers University), 195
Albertson Public Library, 120
Altarama RefTracker, 115, 151
American Library Association
    (ALA), 25, 125, 128
AMP, 161, 166–167
Anhang, Abe, 173, 191
anonymity. *See* user anonymity
AOL Instant Messenger, 55
Apollo program, 160
Arnold, Julie, 26, 41
Arret, Linda, 4, 21, 87, 107
    on chat reference, 76, 95, 96,
        101
    on industry standards, 94
artificial intelligence, 113
Ask-A-Scientist (MAD Scientist),
    110
AskColorado, 4, 8, 11, 20
AskUsNow! *See* Maryland
    AskUsNow!
Association of College and
    Research Libraries (ACRL), 95,
    204

Association of Danish Internet-
    Based Public Library
    Consortia Projects, 149
Association of Research
    Libraries, 170
autonomous agents, 113–114, 127

B

baby boomers, 188
Baker, Sharon L., 25, 40
Balraj, Leela, 50, 53, 73
"bang-for-your-buck" factor, 101
Beavin, Janet, 23, 28, 43
benchmarks, 95, 97–98. *See also*
    performance targets
    comparisons in, 96, 105
    establishing, 94
Bennett, Blythe, 24, 25, 42
bibliographic control, 157
bibliomining, 126
Biblioteksvagten, 134, 136, 140,
    143, 148
    corporate culture of, 145–146
    hours of, 135
    library participation in,
        146–147, 151, 152
    management of, 137, 142,
        147–148
    marketing for, 149–150
    mission of, 137–138
    quality and, 143–144
    service goals of, 141
Blonde, Joe, 75–87, 205

Boneva, Bonka S., 8, 20
Bromberg, Peter, 15, 16, 21, 50, 73
Bunge, Charles A., 40
Bureau of Labor Statistics, 6
Burgoon, Judee K., 37, 43

C

Canadian Association of Research
  Libraries (CARL), 77
canned messages. *See* scripted
  messages
Carnegie Classification of
  Institutions of Higher
  Education, 207
*Carnegie Foundation for the Ad-
  vancement of Teaching*, 207
Carter, David S., 26, 41
Carter, K. A., 27, 41
Center for Advanced Food
  Technology at Cook College
  (Rutgers University), 195
Center for Aerospace Information,
  156
Central Florida Memory, 175
Centralized Configuration
  Management System, 157
Cerritos Library (California), 177
Chan, L., 124, 129
chat reference, 78, 82, 92, 95, 160.
  See also virtual reference
  services; digital reference
  services
  compared with e-mail refer-
    ence, 10, 101–102, 160
  compared with "traditional"
    reference, 26, 37
  costs of, 78, 102–103
  criticism of, 107
  funding of, 20, 78, 152
  hours of, 81, 82–83, 99
  labor intensive nature of, 78
  librarian attitudes toward, 67
  location of, 82

low use of, 86, 95
schedules for, 82–83
session closings in, 38
skills for, 53
software selection for, 151
staff attitudes towards, 84
staff shifts in, 82–83
summer staffing for, 80
technological problems with,
  86
teen perception of, 9
termination of sessions, 30–31,
  35, 118
transaction time and, 103
usage of, 101, 160
user impatience with, 14, 32
value of, 84
volume of questions in, 95, 99,
  115
weekend staffing of, 80
chat rooms, 8, 16
cheat sheets, 53, 57, 64–65, 68,
  164
Chelton, Mary K., 25, 37, 41
Choltco-Devlin, Beverly, 93, 108
"chunking," 112
CKDB (Common Knowledge
  Database), 158
Cleveland Public Library, 99, 101
Clyman, John, 27, 28, 42
co-browsing, 76
Cochenour, John J., 27, 42
Coffman, Steve, 21, 73, 87, 107,
  191
  on chat reference, 4, 76, 95, 96,
    101
  on industry standards, 94
  on virtual reference training,
    50, 51, 69
  on Web searches, 173
College of Information Studies
  (University of Maryland), 49,
  51, 59

Colorado State Library, 11
Colorado Young Adult Advocates in Libraries, 19
communication theory, 24, 38
Competencies for Librarians Serving Youth, 5
complex adaptive systems, 112–113, 127
complexity theory, 112, 127
computer-mediated communication, 27, 37
consortia, 78, 126–127. *See also* cooperative reference
continuing education credits, 53, 60, 69
contract services. *See* outsourcing
controlled vocabulary, 162
Cooperative Holistic Approach to Retrieving Literature in Engineering and Science (CHARLES), 166
cooperative reference, 8, 48. *See also* consortia
corporate culture. *See* organizational culture
course management software, 53, 60. *See also* specific software packages, i.e. WebCT
cross training, 186
Csikszentmihalyi, Mihaly, 5, 21

D
D'Addario, Kyle P., 27, 43
Daghita, Joan, 57, 73
Danet, Brenda, 27, 41
Danish National Library Authority, 134
Danmarks Radio, 150
data mining, 126
data warehouse. *See* Digital Reference Electronic Warehouse (DREW)
Daugaard, Vera, 133–153, 205

Denmark's Electronic Research Library (DEF), 134
Department of Defense (DoD), 161
desktopstreaming. *See* ExpertCity
Dewdney, Patricia, 24, 25, 35, 41, 43
Dialog, 56
Dickerson, Don, 11, 21
diffusion of innovation, 203
Digital Reference Education Initiative (DREI), 159
Digital Reference Electronic Warehouse (DREW), 114, 118, 126, 205
autonomous agents in, 127
goals of, 110–111, 121
schema of, 121–123, 125
digital reference services, 114, 126, 134, 203. *See also* virtual reference services; chat reference
archived transactions of, 110, 128
Dinkelacker, Jamie, 159, 167
"disappearing user," 30
"disconfirming" behavior, 32–33, 34–35
distance education, 58, 60, 61, 70. *See also* online training
drop-out rates and, 62
student dissatisfaction with, 63
Docutek VRL Plus, 115
Doezema, June C., 161, 167
Dudey, Kathryn, 57, 73

E
e-mail reference, 10, 101–102
Early, Charles, 155–166, 205
eAssist NetAgent, 115
eDialog24, 151
Electronic Power Research Institute (EPRI), 160

electronic reference. *See* virtual reference

emoticons, 8, 27, 37

Endres, Sarah, 155–166, 205

escorting, 76

evaluation, 24, 26, 92, 126

evidence-based librarianship, 126

experiential learning, 199

expert systems, 113

ExpertCity, 115

experts, 119, 122

F

fact shifting, 112

Fagan, Jody Condit, 24, 25, 26, 43

Fallows, Deborah, 174, 191

Find It Now (service), 92

Finkelhor, David, 22

firewalls, 63, 64, 71

flaming, 32, 33, 45

Florida Virtual School, 8

focus groups, 9, 11

Fogh, Morten, 133–153, 205

Foley, Marianne, 26, 41

Food and Nutrition Business Informatics and Communication, 194

Food Innovation Center (Rutgers University), 195

Ford, Barbara J., 177, 191

Fox, Barbara J., 161, 167

Fox, Susannah, 173, 191

Fritch, John W., 176, 185, 191

G

Gandhi, Smiti, 160, 167

Generation Y, 189, 190

Giedd, Jay N., 6, 21

Goddard How To Get It Guide, 163, 165, 166

Goddard Space Flight Center. *See* NASA Goddard Space Flight Center

Goetsch, Lori, 203, 207, 208

Goldblatt, Lee, 166, 205

Google, 170, 174

Google Answers, 110

Greene, Louise W., 3–20, 21, 205

Greenfield, Patricia Marks, 7, 21, 22

Gross, Elisheva, 22

Gross, Madeline M., 160, 167

Gross, Melissa, 26, 41, 107, 108

on metrics, 92, 93, 94

Guidelines for Behavioral Performance of Reference and Information Services Professionals (RUSA *Guidelines*). *See* Reference and User Services Association (RUSA)

H

Hamburger, Susan D., 21

Hanes, Lewis F., 159, 160

Harris, Lydia, 51, 73

Harvard Graduate School of Education, 204

Heekin, Janet, 57, 73

High-Level Thesaurus Project (HILT), 124

Hirko, Buff, 51, 73

Hirsh, Sandra, 159, 167

Hoffman, Robert R., 159, 160, 167

Holland, John H., 112, 113, 129

Homework Help (service), 92, 104

homework questions, 12, 18

Horn, Judy, 51, 73

How to Get it Guide (DoD), 161

Hubble Space Telescope, 156

Huber, Susan, 91–107

HumanClick. *See* LivePerson

Hutchison, Deb, 91–107, 205

I

IM. *See* instant messaging

Information Institute of
     Syracuse, 204
information literacy, 194, 195
instant messaging, 7, 26, 27, 173.
     See also chat reference
Internet Public Library (IPL), 26
interpersonal communication,
     24, 27, 38–40
     relational barriers in, 29, 30
     relational disconnect/failure
        to build rapport, 30, 31–32
relational facilitators in, 29
Ithaca College Library, 158

J
Jackson, Donald D., 23, 28, 43
Janes, Joseph, 26, 41, 107, 176,
     191
     census of digital reference
        and, 95, 96, 170
     on industry standards, 94
Jantz, Ron, 158, 167, 205
Japzon, Andrea, 155–166
job descriptions, 83, 86
Johnson, Corey, 24, 41
Johnson, Denise J., 37, 42
Jones, Patrick, 37, 41

K
Kaske, Neal, 26, 41, 44, 95, 108
     on industry standards, 94
Kasowitz, Abby, 24, 25, 42
Katz, William A., 160, 167
Kaysen, Debra, 21
Kiesler, Sara, 20
King County Library System
     (Washington), 104
King, Donald W., 198, 201
knowledge bases, 110, 124, 159
     as training tools, 166
     benefits of, 165, 166
     creation of, 128, 161–162
     limitations of, 111–112

quality of, 163
search types in, 163–164
Kommuneinformation, 151
Kortz, Laura, 3–20, 205
Kozuch, Patricia, 21
Kraemer, Elizabeth W., 53, 73
Krag, Susanne Dalsgaard, 153
Kraut, Robert E., 20, 22

L
Lancaster, F. Wilfrid, 25, 40
Lance, Keith, 11, 21
Lange, Nicholas, 21
Lankes, R. David, 42, 107, 108,
     129, 207
     on complexity theory, 112
     on digital reference
        evaluation, 24, 25
     on DREW, 109–128
     on metrics, 92, 93, 94
     research agenda and, 204,
        205
Larson, Reed, 5, 21
learning styles, 68
Lenhart, Amanda, 173, 192
librarians, 18, 19, 26, 32, 38, 152
Library of Congress, 123, 129,
     204
library policies, 84
Library Research Services, 11
licensed databases, 60
Liebowitz, Jay, 159, 167
Lilly, Erica, 159, 167
Linux, 167
Lipow, Anne Grodzins, 50, 73,
     177, 185, 191
LivePerson, 115
Love, Gail, 27, 38, 42
LSSI Samuel Swett Green
     Award, 26, 29
LSSI, 51, 72, 151. *See also* Virtual
     Reference Toolkit (VRT)
Luther, Judy, 6, 20

M

Maczewski, Mechthild, 7, 21
Madden, Mary, 173, 192
management information
    systems, 126
Mandernack, Scott B., 176, 185,
    191
Mariner, Vince, 8, 21
marketing, 11, 149–150, 174
    at Vancouver Public Library,
        104
Marsteller, Matthew R., 94, 95,
    102, 108
Maryland AskUsNow! (service),
    4, 9, 28, 29, 39, 100
Massey-Burzio, Virginia, 11, 21
Matthews, Anne J., 35, 42
McClure, Charles R., 25, 41, 42,
    107, 108
    on evaluation, 26
    on metrics, 92, 93, 94
McCulloch, Emma, 124, 129
McNeil, Beth, 37, 42
Meola, Mark, 53, 73, 76, 87
Merchant, Guy, 8, 21
metadata, 111, 114
Metz, Cade, 27, 28, 42
"millennials," 6
Mitchell, Kimberly J., 22
Mon, Lori, 26, 41
Morris, Sharon, 3–20, 205
multitasking, 8, 10, 67, 83
Multnomah Public Libraries
    (Oregon), 158
MYSQL, 166

N

NASA Goddard Space Flight
    Center, 155, 156, 157, 160, 161
National Center for Education,
    173
National Institutes of Mental
    Health, 6, 21

National Library of Canada, 204
National Library of Medicine,
    124, 129
National Oceanic and Atmos-
    pheric Administration, 156
National Telecommunications
    and Information Admin-
    istration, 6, 21
natural language processing, 125
NetRef, 123
Neuhaus, Paul, 94, 95, 108
neural nets, 113
New Brunswick Campus
    Libraries (Rutgers University),
    158
Nicholson, Dennis
Nicholson, Scott, 124, 129
Nielsen, Ellen, 133–153, 205
Nilsen, Kirsti, 25, 26, 42
NISO AZ. See NetRef
nonverbal communication, 26,
    28, 29, 37, 38
Novotny, Eric, 25, 42

O

OLIVE, 174, 182–184. See also
    Orange County Library
    System
Online Computer Library Center
    (OCLC), 129, 159, 204. See also
    QuestionPoint
online publishing, 198
online training, 51, 57, 68. See also
    training; distance education
    assessment of, 52
    benefits of, 50
    technical support for, 59, 68
online tutorials, 57, 64–65, 66
Open Ask A Question, 115
Open Conference Software
    (OCS), 198, 199
Open Journal System (OJS), 197,
    198, 199

open source software, 128, 197, 198, 201
Orange County Library System, 171, 174–175, 187. *See also* OLIVE
  decline in reference questions at, 170, 172, 176
  reorganization of reference at, 186
Orange County Planning Division, 171, 191
organizational culture, 76, 84, 145–146
outsourcing, 85

P
Patriot Act, 124
patron behavior. *See* user behavior
PBS Frontline, 6, 21
PDAs. *See* pocket PCs
peer pressure, 84
Perez, Ernest, 158, 167
performance targets. *See also* quality; benchmarks
  at Vancouver Public Library, 96, 99, 100, 101, 103
  definition of, 93
  establishment of, 93–94, 98
  transaction time and, 103
Pew Internet and American Life Project, 7, 21, 173, 174
PHP LiveSupport, 115
PHP scripting language, 166
Pittsburgh Public Library, 177
pocket PCs, 175, 179
podcasts, 173
Pragmatics of Human Communication, 28
prank questions, 15, 16
privacy, 29, 124–125
Public Knowledge Project (PKP), 197, 198

Public Library Data Service, 108
pushing pages, 55, 57
Pye, Michele, 91–107, 205

Q
QABuilder, 115
QandA NJ, 4, 9, 15, 50
quality, 143–144, 204. *See also* benchmarks; performance targets
quality standard, 93
QuestionPoint, 115
  knowledge base of, 110, 122, 159
questions, 12, 14, 15, 16–17. *See also* prank questions
  routing, 118
  threading of, 123, 124
  transaction time of, 103
QuestLine, 172, 174, 182, 187
Quinn, Amy, 20

R
Radford, Marie L., 21, 23–40, 42, 205
  on difficult patrons, 14, 18
Raine, Lee, 173, 192
Rajapakse, Jagata C., 21
Rapaport, Judith, 21
Ready Reference Database, 158
Reference and User Services Association (RUSA), 42, 84, 87
  Guidelines document, 25
reference authoring, 128
reference desk, 176, 177, 178, 190
reference interview, 16, 55–56, 205
reference transactions, 124
  at reference desk, 158, 177
  classification of, 123
  data collection and, 116–118, 119
repeat users, 104
Rettig, James, 177, 180, 192
Reynolds, Lindsey, 7, 22
Rezabek, Landra L., 27, 43

Rice, Ronald E., 27, 38, 43
Robinson, Kathryn, 169–191, 205
Rogers, Everett M., 203, 207, 208
role playing, 53, 54, 55, 58, 69
Ronan, Jana, 25, 43, 73, 76, 87
    on interpersonal communica-
        tion, 38, 40
    on multitasking, 67
Rosenbaum-Tamari, Yehudit, 27,
    40
Ross, Catherine S., 24, 25, 35, 40,
    43
Ross, Mary Bucher, 73
roving reference, 176–177, 187–188
RSS feeds, 175, 191
Rubin, Rhea, 37, 43
rudeness, 30, 33, 38
    tips for handling, 14, 17–18, 32,
        45–46
Ruedenberg-Wright, Lucia, 27, 40
Ruffner, Malissa, 49–72, 205
Rumbaugh, Paula, 122
Ruppel, Margie, 24, 25, 26, 43
Rutgers Food Policy Institute, 195
Rutgers University, 193
Rutgers University Libraries, 194

S

Salem, Joseph, 50, 53
San Diego State University, 158
School of Communications,
    Information & Library Studies
    (Rutgers), 195
Scientific and Technical
    Information Program, 156
scripted messages, 17
search engines, 173
SearchEngine Watch, 173
Seattle Public Library, 177–178
Sheets, Janet E., 53, 73
Shiri, Ali, 124, 129
Shiu, Eulynn, 173, 192
Shklovski, Irina, 20

Simpson, A. Rae, 22
Sloan, Bernie, 25, 43
Smith, Kitty, 37, 43
Snell, John W., 21
software, 56, 59, 63, 71
    24/7, 28, 29, 115, 159
    Altarama RefTracker, 115, 151
    AMP, 161, 166–167
    AOL Instant Messenger, 55
    authentication issues in, 56, 71
    eDialog24, 151
    firewalls, 63, 64, 71
    Linux, 167
    MYSQL, 166
    Online Journal System (OJS),
        197, 198, 199
    Open Conference Software
        (OCS), 198, 199
    open source, 128, 197, 198, 201
    Solaris, 167
    vendors, 72
    Viewlet, 53, 57
    Virtual Reference Toolkit (VRT),
        53–55, 57, 62, 72, 151
    WebCT, 53, 54, 55, 59
Solaris, 167
Spors, Kelly K., 177, 192
staff, 81–82, 84, 185
    costs of, 4
    cross training of, 186
    impact of retirements on, 160
    scheduling, 85
    workloads of, 77, 83, 86
staffing, 77–78, 79, 80, 135
    at reference desk, 81
    for chat reference, 76, 82, 83, 86
    outsourcing and, 85
Statistical Report, 96, 99, 101
*Statistics, Measures, and Quality
    Standards for Assessing Digital
    Reference Library Services:
    Guidelines and Procedures*, 93
Steinberg, Laurence, 5, 22

Stormont, Sam, 53, 73, 76, 87
Stover, Mark, 158, 167
Stratigos, Anthea, 176, 185, 190, 192
Strauch, Barbara, 6, 22
Strouse, Roger, 176, 185, 190, 192
Subrahmanyam, Kaveri, 7, 21, 22
suicide, 18
surveys, 11, 52
Sweet, Marianne, 9, 14, 16

T

24/7 Reference service, 28, 29, 115, 159
tablet PCs, 181
tacit knowledge, 158, 160
teenagers, 4, 5, 7, 8, 20
  information-seeking behavior of, 6, 9–10, 12
  strategies for working with, 19–20, 37
telephone reference, 60
telephone training, 53, 57–58, 68. *See also* training
Tenopir, Carol, 56, 73, 198, 201
"thank you" messages, 13, 26
Thompson, Joseph, 21, 22, 37, 42
  on difficult patrons, 14, 18
  on teen patrons, 9, 11
threading. *See* questions
time management, 70, 185
Todd, Mark, 27, 28, 42
"train the trainer," 50
training, 50, 51, 66, 104. *See also* online training; distance education
  by software vendors, 50, 56, 72
  by telephone, 53, 57–58
  cheat sheets, 49, 53, 57, 64–65, 68
  complications in, 50, 51, 56, 70–71
  effectiveness of, 63–66

  hands-on practice and, 51, 53, 55–56, 62, 68–69
  on software, 55, 71
  role playing in, 53, 54, 55, 58, 69
  satisfaction with, 63–65
transcripts, 19, 23, 25, 160, 205
  as training tools, 53, 55, 159
Tucker, James Cory, 50, 73
Tunender, Heather, 51, 73
Turner, Anne M., 37, 43
Turner, Carol, 76, 87
Tutor.com, 72, 115, 151
Tynes, Brendesha, 22, 71
typographical errors, 36

U

UCLA Internet Report, 6, 22
uncontrolled keywords, 162
University of British Columbia, 197
University of Maryland, 49, 51, 57
USA Patriot. *See* Patriot Act
U.S. Census Bureau, 6, 22
user anonymity, 8, 10
user behavior, 30, 32–33, 35, 38, 45

V

Vaituzis, Catherine A., 21
Vancouver Public Library, 92, 103
  costs of chat reference at, 102–103
  performance targets at, 96, 99, 100–101, 103, 104
  repeat users at, 104, 105
Vauss, Yolanda C., 21
vector-based information retrieval, 112
video conferencing, 174–175, 184–185
  types of questions in, 182

Viewlet software, 53, 57
virtual collaboratory, 193–194,
    197–199
    assessment of, 199–200
virtual learning communities,
    197–199
virtual reference, 51, 83, 95. *See
    also* chat reference
Virtual Reference 1.0, 51
Virtual Reference Desk
    Conference, 24, 204
virtual reference services. *See also*
    digital reference services; chat
    reference
    archived transactions in, 159
    coordinators for, 85
    growth of, 86
    at Orange County Library
        System, 172, 174–175, 187
    quality of, 204
    staff participation in, 84
    teen perceptions of, 13
Virtual Reference Toolkit (VRT),
    54, 57, 72
    hands-on experience and, 53,
        55, 62
visual cues, 183
Vocera communications system,
    179, 180–181
voice recognition software,
    180
VRD Conference. *See* Virtual
    Reference Desk Conference

W
Waldrop, M. Mitchell, 112, 129
Walther, Joseph B., 27, 37, 38, 43
Ward, David, 53, 73
Ware, Susan, 102, 108
Washington State Library, 51
Watzlawick, Paul, 23, 28, 43
Web-based training. *See* online
    training
WebCT, 53, 54, 55, 59
Weingand, Darlene E., 37, 43
Wenk, Karen, 193, 205
White, Marilyn Domas, 26, 44,
    95, 108, 203
    on industry standards, 94
Whitlatch, JoBell, 25, 44
Willinsky, John, 197, 201
Wilson, Myoung C., 176, 192
wireless technology, 169, 178,
    179–180
Wolak, Janis, 7, 22
Workgroup for Electronic Data
    Interchange, 129

Y
Young Adult Library Service
    Association (YALSA), 5, 22
young adults. *See* teenagers
youth development. *See*
    adolescent development

Z
Zeng, M., 124, 129

About the Editors

R. DAVID LANKES

R. David Lankes, Ph.D., is director of the Information Institute of Syracuse (IIS) and an associate professor at Syracuse (N.Y.) University's School of Information Studies. The IIS houses the Gateway to Educational Materials (GEM), the Virtual Reference Desk (VRD), and AskNSDL (National Science Digital Library). Lankes' research is in education information and digital reference services. He has authored, co-authored, or edited five books and written numerous book chapters and journal articles on the Internet and digital reference.

MARILYN DOMAS WHITE

Marilyn Domas White has experience related to studying questions and questioning behavior in a range of settings, including reference interviews, digital reference services, and electronic lists; questions as a factor in Web searching; and evaluation of information services. She has published in digital reference services and has supervised various student projects analyzing questions in this environment and search logs. She regularly teaches in the area of information access and communications at the College of Information Studies at the University of Maryland.

EILEEN G. ABELS

Eileen G. Abels, Ph.D., is an associate professor at the College of Information Studies (CLIS) and an affiliate associate professor at the Robert H. Smith School of Business at the University of Maryland. She teaches in the area of information access and has developed an online course titled E-reference. She also oversaw the development of a series of online workshops on virtual reference. Her research interests focus on the value of library and information services, business information needs and services, and digital reference.

SAIRA N. HAQUE

Saira N. Haque is a doctoral student at the School of Information Studies at Syracuse University. Her research interests are in health informatics and organizational information security. She is a Diplomate of the American College of Healthcare Executives and has held a variety of leadership positions in academic medical centers and consulting firms. Going forward, she plans on combining her research interests with her practical knowledge.

About the
Contributors

JOE BLONDE

Joe Blonde is coordinator of the Live Electronic Reference Working Group at Concordia University Libraries in Montreal, a group that manages the Ask A Librarian chat reference service. He also represents the library on the Conference des recteurs et des principaux des universités du Québec (CREPUQ) provincial working group developing collaborative initiatives in electronic reference. Mr. Blonde is a reference librarian engaged in collection and liaison work with the Faculty of Engineering and Computer Science.

VERA DAUGAARD

Vera Daugaard graduated from the Royal School of Library and Information Science, Denmark. in 1979. She has been the reference librarian at the Herning Central Library since 1979. Vera has served as the project manager for www.biblioteksvagten.dk since its inception in 1999.

CHARLES EARLY

Charles Early has been the engineering librarian at NASA/ Goddard Space Flight Center since 1994. His previous professional experience includes work as engineering librarian at the University of Notre Dame, head of Engineering Reference and engineering bibliographer at Stanford University, and head of Collection Development at the Milton S. Eisenhower Library at

Johns Hopkins University. He has an M.L.S. from Indiana University and an M.S. in physics from St. Louis University. Charles is an employee of Information International Associates, Inc., prime contractor for the Goddard Library project

SARAH ENDRES

Sarah Endres graduated in 1994 with a B.S. in mathematics from Columbia Union College, and a master's of library science in 1996 from the University of Maryland. After obtaining her M.L.S., she held a variety of library positions throughout the Washington D.C. metropolitan area for several months before starting a contracting library position with the Technology Administration, U.S. Department of Commerce. After five years as a solo librarian, she began working for Zimmerman Associates, Inc., in the library at the NASA Goddard Space Flight Center. Continuing her enjoyment of diversity in her job, she works in several areas of the library, including cataloging, reference, and systems.

MORTEN FOGH

Marten Fogh graduated from the Royal School of Library and Information Science, Denmark, in 1982. He has held director positions at the Videbaek Library and Vejle Central Library. He currently is the director of the Herning Central Library. He has been the managing board president for www.biblioteksvagten.dk since 2004 and the managing board president for the Association of Danish Internet-based Public Library Consortia Projects since 2001.

LOUISE W. GREENE

Louise W. Greene has been the head of the Reference Department at Anne Arundel Community College since 1998. She received an M.L.S. from the University of Maryland at College Park and an M.S. in sociology from Texas A & M. Anne Arundel Community College is one of two community colleges in the Maryland AskUsNow consortium and one of five academic libraries participating in the statewide virtual reference consortium.

Having raised three teenagers single-handedly, she can LOL about this topic.

DEB HUTCHISON

Deb Hutchison coordinates the day-to-day operations of Vancouver Public Library's two live online information services: Find It Now and Homework Help. Her areas of interest include information literacy, human-computer interaction, and the design of information systems. She has an M.L.I.S. from the University of British Columbia, and an M.A. from Queen's University. One of the more interesting jobs she's had was a three-week internship at BBC Television, where, among other things, she researched celebrities who had lost their luggage.

ANDREA JAPZON

Andrea C. Japzon earned an M.L.S. from Florida State University in 1994 and moved to New York City the same year to begin working as a librarian at the New York Public Library. In 1999, she joined the library faculty at Hunter College of the City University of New York. While at Hunter, she completed an M.A. in geography. She was awarded the 2001 fellowship from the Society for Woman Geographers for her thesis research, "A Regional Analysis of Public Library Use in New York City." In March 2004, she began working at the NASA Goddard Space Flight Center Library and currently serves as the deputy project manager for the subcontractor of the library project, Zimmerman Associates, Inc.

LAURA KORTZ

Laura Kortz is virtual services librarian at New Jersey City University, in Jersey City. She serves as project manager for the library's participation in Q and A NJ, New Jersey's 24/7 online reference service. She is currently pursuing an M.A. in Counseling Psychology at NJCU and earned an M.L.S. from Rutgers University in 1998. She has been chatting online since 1993 and realized even back then that chat and reference would be a good combination.

SHARON MORRIS

Sharon Morris is the coordinator of the award-winning Ask-Colorado collaborative virtual reference service and a *Library Journal* 2005 Mover and Shaker. Since the launch of AskColorado in September 2003, she and other online reference staff have assisted (and angsted over) teens who access the service. Prior to joining AskColorado, she held positions as assistant to the dean of the Emporia State University Library School, acquisitions librarian for the Colorado State Library, product manager for library automation software at the CARL Corporation, and youth services librarian at the Denver Public Library. She has an M.L.S. from Emporia State University.

SCOTT NICHOLSON

Scott Nicholson, Ph.D., is a faculty member at the School of Information Studies at Syracuse University. His main research area is the creation of models and measures to aid managers in evaluating and managing digital library services. His main tool is bibliomining, or data mining, for libraries, which allows him to discover patterns in low-level data. He is a research scientist for the Information Institute of Syracuse, where he works on the future of the management and automation of digital reference functions.

ELLEN NIELSEN

Ellen Nielsen graduated from the Royal School of Library and Information Science of Denmark in 1982. She has been a reference librarian at Aarhus School of Business since 1982. In addition, she has been the project manager for the academic sector libraries in www.biblioteksvagten.dk since 2003.

MICHELE PYE

Michele Pye is the coordinator of the Virtual Library Department at Vancouver Public Library, and oversees subscription databases, virtual services, and the development of the public

Web site, among other responsibilities. She is the co-author of "Putting the User First in Virtual Information Services" (*Public Libraries* Nov/Dec 2003). Her areas of interest include Web site usability, leadership, and building relationships between the library and its communities. She has an M.L.I.S. from the University of British Columbia.

MARIE L. RADFORD

Marie L. Radford, Ph.D., is a faculty member at Rutgers University, SCILS. Her research interests are interpersonal aspects of reference service (in face-to-face and virtual environments), evaluation of e-resources and services, cultural studies, and media stereotypes of librarians. She makes frequent presentations at communication and library conferences and has published in *College & Research Libraries, Library Quarterly, Library Trends, JELIS,* and the *Journal of Academic Librarianship.* Her books are *The Reference Encounter: Interpersonal Communication in the Academic Library* (ACRL/ALA, 1999) and *Web Research: Selection, Evaluation, and Citing* (Allyn & Bacon, 2002, 2nd ed. to be published in 2006).

KATHRYN ROBINSON

Kathryn Robinson is the head of the Reference Division of the Orange County (Fla.) Library System. Along with the rest of the reference and information team she is responsible for information services for adults and youth at the main library, including mobile services and QuestLine, with information services provided by phone, chat, e-mail and videoconferencing. Kathryn received her M.L.S. from Florida State University.

MALISSA RUFFNER

Malissa Ruffner began her working life as a computer programmer, then graduated from the University of Maryland School of Law in 1985. She served as staff attorney at the ACLU of Maryland and as a private school director for an institution she helped to establish. After receiving her M.L.S. degree from the College of Information Studies (CLIS) at the University of Maryland in 2002, Malissa established InfoProjects LLC, and, as an independent information professional, works as a researcher, archivist, records manager, coordinator for a virtual reference workshop series, and a teaching assistant for an e-reference course.

KAREN WENK

Karen Wenk, as science digital initiatives librarian at Rutgers, has primary responsibility for digital library projects related to the sciences and possesses strong programming, Web-design, and graphics skills. As one of the project investigators, she is working with Cook College students in the development of the Virtual Collaboratory.